Maritime INNS & RESTAURANTS COOKBOOK

Elaine Elliot and Virginia Lee

Formac Publishing Company Limited
Halifax, 1990

Edited by Susan Williams

Canadian Cataloguing in Publication Data
Elliot, Elaine, 1939 -
The Maritime Inns and Restaurants Cookbook
ISBN 0-88780-079-3
1. Cookery, Canadian — Maritime Provinces.
2 Restaurants, lunch rooms, etc. — Maritime Provinces — Directories. 3. Hotels, taverns, etc. — Maritime Provinces — Directories.
I. Lee, Virginia, 1947 - II. Title.
TX715.6.E44 1990 641.5'09715 C90-097658-6

Formac Publishing Limited
5502 Atlantic Street
Halifax, N.S.
B3H 1G4

Printed and bound in Canada.

Contents

This book is dedicated to our husbands, Robert and Mel, and our families, with love.

Introduction

We may live without poetry, music and art;
We may live without conscience, and live without heart;
We may live without friends, we may live without books;
But civilized man cannot live without cooks.

He may live without books, — what is knowledge but grieving?
He may live without hope, — what is hope but deceiving?
He may live without love, — what is passion but pining?
But where is the man that can live without dining?
Owen Meredith (1831 - 1891)

The Maritime Provinces have long had a reputation for warm hospitality and fine traditional cooking. It is with pride that we acknowledge the quality chefs and establishments of the region by presenting some of their recipes to you, the reader.

We cannot begin to thank our contributors for the generous support and encouragement given to us. It was a pleasure meeting with them, often over a cup of tea or coffee, and usually at a time when they were busy. Nevertheless, our hosts took time to talk, give us a tour of their establishments and share anecdotes. While we enjoyed our personal contact with these restauranteurs, we also recognize the time they shared with us, over the phone, answering our many queries.

You may use this book in several ways: to randomly select and try a recipe, to prepare a memorable food experience from a favourite spot or as a tour guide to help you sample the cuisine of the region's inns and restaurants.

We have personally tested all the recipes and adjusted them to serve four to six people. We have also included information about the contributing inns and restaurants, a map showing their locations, as well as a metric conversion guide.

It is our hope that this book will provide you with many memorable dining experiences. Bon appetit!

Elaine Elliot and Virginia Lee

New Brunswick
Prince Edward Island
Nova Scotia
New Mills
Grande-Anse
Fredericton
Gagetown
Sackville
Rothesay
St. Martins
St. Andrews
North Head
Grand Manan Island
O'Leary
Brackley Beach
Stanhope
Souris
Bay Fortune
Victoria
Vernon River
Charlottetown
Lorneville
Amherst
Pictou
Parrsboro
Ingonish Beach
Margaree Valley
Baddeck
Sydney Mines
Sherbrooke
Liscomb Mills
Wolfville
Waverley
Annapolis Royal
South Milford
Chester
Dartmouth
Smith's Cove
Marriott's Cove
Halifax
Mahone Bay
Digby
Lunenburg
Hebron
Shelburne

New Brunswick

Fredericton
Benoit's
Gagetown
Steamers Stop Inn
Grande-Anse
La Poissonière Restaurant
Grand Manan Island
The Compass Rose Inn
New Mills
Heron Country Inn
Rothesay
Shadow Lawn Country Inn
Sackville
The Marshlands Inn
St. Andrews
The Algonquin Inn
The Rossmount Inn
Tara Maor Inn
St. Martins
The Quaco Inn

Nova Scotia

Annapolis Royal
The Garrison House Inn
Baddeck
Inverary Inn Resort
Telegraph House
Chester
The Captain's House
The Galley
Dartmouth
La Perla
Digby
The Pines Resort Hotel
Halifax
Halliburton House Inn
O'Carroll's Restaurant
Silver Spoon Restaurants
Upper Deck Restaurant
Hebron
The Manor Inn
Ingonish Beach
Keltic Lodge
Liscombe Mills
Liscombe Lodge
Lorneville
Amherst Shore Country Inn
Lunenburg
Boscowan Inn
The Compass Rose
The Lunenburg Inn
Mahone Bay
The Inlet Café
Zwicker's Inn
Margaree Valley
The Normaway Inn
Pictou
New Consulate Restaurant
Parrsboro
The Maple Inn
Shelburne
Cooper's Inn
Sherbrooke
The Bright House
Smith's Cove
Harbourview Inn
Mountain Gap Inn
South Milford
The Milford House
Sydney Mines
Gowrie House
Waverley
Inn on the Lake
Wolfville
The Blomidon Inn
Chez La Vigne
Tattingstone Inn
Victoria's Historic Inn

Prince Edward Island

Bay Fortune
The Inn at the Bay Fortune
Brackley Beach
Shaw's Hotel
Charlottetown
The Dundee Arms Inn
Stanhope by the Sea
O'Leary
The West Point Lighthouse
Vernon River
The Garden Restaurant
Victoria
Victoria Village Inn

Appetizers

Antipasto

Harbourview Inn

¼ cup vegetable oil
1 small jar pimento, drained
1 green pepper, diced
1 7oz. can flaked tuna, drained
1 can mushroom stems and pieces, drained
1 cup mustard style hot dog relish
1 dozen or more stuffed olives, sliced
1 dozen Kalamata style black olives, pitted and sliced
2 cups tomato ketchup
1 small bottle chili sauce
2 garlic cloves, crushed
1/4 teaspoon cinnamon
1 can anchovy fillets, drained and chopped
½ cup vinegar

In a large saucepan heat oil and sauté diced pimento and green pepper for 3 - 5 minutes, being careful not to brown. Add all the other ingredients and simmer 10 - 15 minutes. Cool and store in covered jars, refrigerated, up to 6 months. Serve on assorted crackers. Yields six 8 oz. jars.

Potted Cheese

Zwicker's Inn

8 oz. medium Cheddar cheese
1/4 cup (generous) softened butter
2 modest pinches ground mace
3 tablespoons sherry, not too dry

Bring cheese and butter to room temperature. Drop broken pieces of cheese into the feeder tube of a food processor and process into small bits. Add remaining ingredients to processor bowl and process *only* until well mixed. Will keep for many weeks refrigerated. Serve at room temperature with crackers. Yields 1 1/4 cups.

Mackerel Seviche

La Poissonnière

1 mackerel, cleaned, filleted and cut into bite-sized pieces
1 medium Spanish onion, sliced in thin rings
3/4 cup fresh lime juice
juice of 1 orange
juice of 1 lemon
1/4 teaspoon red pepper flakes
1/4 teaspoon horseradish
1 teaspoon sugar
1 teaspoon salt
dash of white pepper
1 bay leaf
fresh parsley, chopped

Prepare mackerel and onion. Combine juices, pepper flakes, horseradish, sugar, salt, pepper and bay leaf. In a glass bowl alternate mackerel and onion rings. Pour juice mixture over fish and onion making sure it is completely submerged. Cover dish and refrigerate at least 5 hours or up to 24 hours, turning fish once or twice (lime juice will "cook" the raw fish). Drain and serve as an appetizer garnished with parsley. Serves 4-6.

Spinach Quiche

The Bright House

pastry to line a 10-inch quiche dish
8-10 oz. sharp Cheddar cheese, grated
1 12 oz. package fresh spinach, washed and stems removed
1 cup milk
1/2 small onion
4 eggs
1/2 cup sour cream
1/2 cup evaporated milk
2 tablespoons flour
salt and pepper to taste
generous grating of nutmeg
pinch paprika

Spread half the grated cheese over the bottom of prepared quiche pastry. In a blender or food processor purée the washed spinach, milk and onion. Pour into a large bowl and beat in the eggs, sour cream, evaporated milk, flour, salt, pepper and nutmeg. Pour into quiche pan, sprinkle with remaining cheese and paprika. Bake for 10 minutes in a preheated 425°F oven. Reduce heat to 325°F and bake an additional 30-35 minutes or until set. Let stand a few minutes before serving. Serves 8-10 as an appetizer or 4-6 as a luncheon dish.

Smoked Salmon Appetizer Plate

The Tattingstone Inn

1/4 lb. smoked salmon, thinly sliced
4 sprigs fresh dill weed
4 teaspoons finely diced Spanish or Bermuda onion
16-20 capers
4 slices cream cheese, optional

Place 4-5 slices of smoked salmon on each plate. Garnish with dill sprigs, a teaspoon of onion, 4-5 capers and a thin slice of cream cheese, if desired. Serves 4.

Escargot Stuffed Mushroom Caps

The Manor Inn

24 mushroom caps, medium size
24 escargot
4 tablespoons garlic butter
1 tablespoon white wine
1 tablespoon lemon juice

Clean mushroom caps and pat dry. Rinse escargot under cold water and drain well. In a saucepan melt 1/2 of the garlic butter, add the wine and lemon juice. Add mushrooms and sauté gently over low heat 3-4 minutes until softened.

Divide mushrooms and pan drippings between four heatproof dishes, place escargot in mushrooms, top with remaining garlic butter and broil until bubbly. Serves 4.

Garlic Butter
2-3 garlic cloves
1/4 cup butter

Boil garlic cloves in small saucepan in water for 5 minutes, drain. Crush garlic and mix well with softened butter. Makes 1/4 cup or 4 tablespoons garlic butter.

Stuffed Mushrooms

New Consulate Restaurant

24 mushrooms, large enough to stuff
2 tablespoons butter
1 medium onion, finely chopped
1/4 cup finely chopped green pepper
1 garlic clove
2 oz. pepperoni (1/4 cup)
3 tablespoons Parmesan cheese
1 tablespoon chopped fresh parsley
1/4 teaspoon oregano
1/2 teaspoon salt
dash pepper
1/2 cup Ritz crackers
1/3 cup chicken broth

Wash mushrooms, remove stems and pat dry with paper towels. Chop mushroom stems and reserve. Melt butter in a skillet, add onion, green pepper, garlic and mushroom stems and sauté until soft.

In a food processor coarsely chop pepperoni. Add onion mixture, cheese, parsley, seasonings and crackers to food processor and chop coarsely. Do not purée. Return pepperoni mixture to the skillet along with broth and cook until tender but not brown.

Fill mushroom caps with pepperoni mixture. Pour enough water into a baking dish to barely cover the bottom and place caps in the water. Bake, uncovered, in a preheated 325°F oven for 25 minutes. Extra stuffing may be placed on French bread rounds and placed under the broiler to heat. Serves 4-6.

Solomon Gundy Appetizer Plates

The Lunenburg Inn

6 large lettuce leaves, washed and trimmed
8 oz. jar Solomon Gundy (marinated herring)
12 tablespoons sour cream
18 round whole wheat crackers
3 medium celery stocks, cut in 4-inch strips
1 medium carrot, peeled and julienned
1 large tomato, sliced into wedges

Cover the centres of 6 serving plates with lettuce leaves. Distribute drained herring pieces between the plates and place 2 tablespoons of sour cream beside the fish. Overlap the crackers on one side of the plates while distributing the celery and carrot sticks on the other side. Garnish with wedges of tomato. Yields 6 appetizer servings.

Mussels Bourgignon

Upper Deck Restaurant

32 large mussels
1/4 cup butter
1 large or 2 small cloves garlic, crushed
1 teaspoon parsley flakes
1/2 cup dry bread crumbs
1/3 teaspoon salt
1/3 teaspoon white pepper
1/2 teaspoon oregano

Wash and remove beards from the mussels, discarding any that are open or have broken shells. With a paring knife cut open mussels, scoop both halves to one side of mussel shell, making sure the cartilage is cut in the back. Place mussels on a cookie sheet.

Prepare garlic butter by whipping together the butter, crushed garlic cloves and parsley. Place 1/3 teaspoon garlic butter on each mussel. Mix the bread crumbs with salt, pepper and oregano. Sprinkle on each mussel. Bake at 375°F for 2-3 minutes. Serves 4.

Shrimp Avocado Cocktail

Inn on the Lake

2 small avocados
1 cup cubed fresh pineapple
1 1/2 cups (12 oz.) baby shrimp
1/2 cup egg-based mayonnaise
2 tablespoons ketchup
1 tablespoon brandy
salt and pepper to taste
lettuce and radicchio leaves
4-6 slices lemon
4-6 slices lime

Cut avocados in half, scoop out meat and dice. Combine avocado, pineapple and shrimp and set aside.

Whisk together mayonnaise, ketchup, brandy and seasonings. Toss avocado mixture with sauce and replace in avocado shells. Garnish with lettuce, radicchio, lemon and lime slices. Serves 4 or 6 if mixture is not placed in shells but served on lettuce leaves.

Scallops in Mushroom Cream Sauce

Shadow Lawn Country Inn

2 tablespoons butter
4 green onions, chopped
1/4 lb. mushrooms, sliced
1 large carrot, shredded
1/2 cup milk
2 tablespoons white wine or lemon juice
4 tablespoons Bechamel sauce mix (white sauce mix)
1 lb.scallops
1 cup Swiss cheese, grated (4 oz.)
Fresh parsley, chopped
Lemon wedges

Microwave Method!
In a 2-quart glass casserole, melt butter on high for 1 minute. Add green onions, mushrooms and carrots; cover with plastic wrap, vent and cook on high for 3 minutes.

Whisk milk, wine and Bechamel sauce mix together until well blended and stir into casserole. Cover, vent and cook on high 3 minutes, stirring once.

Stir in scallops, cover, vent and cook on high 2 minutes. Add cheese and gently stir until melted. Spoon into 8 small scallop shells, garnish with parsley and lemon wedges. Serve immediately.

Yields 8 appetizers or 4 main course servings.

Soups

Fisherman's Soup

The Normaway Inn

1 lb. white-fleshed fish (haddock, halibut, etc.)
1/2 lb. shellfish (lobster, scallops, shrimp, etc.)
3/4 cup dry white wine
water
1 1/2 tablespoons olive oil
1 large onion, chopped
1 large garlic clove, minced
2/3 cup diced green pepper
1/2 cup chopped celery stock and leaves
1/3 cup grated carrot
3 tablespoons chopped fresh parsley
1 teaspoon thyme
1/2 teaspoon fennel seed
1 28 oz. can tomatoes, chopped in blender
salt and pepper to taste
1/2 bay leaf
lemon or orange peel (optional)
pinch of saffron (optional)

Poach seafood in white wine and enough water to cover until slightly undercooked. Drain the liquid into a saucepan through a colander and simmer until reduced to one half. Remove bones and shells from the seafood and reserve.

In a large soup kettle heat the oil and sauté the onion, garlic, green pepper, celery, carrots, 1 1/2 tablespoons of the parsley, thyme and fennel. Cover and "sweat" the vegetables for 5 minutes. Add the tomatoes, fish stock, salt, pepper, bay leaf and optional seasonings and simmer for 15 minutes. Add seafood and remaining parsley, adjust seasonings and simmer 5 minutes more. Yields 6-8 servings.

Cream of Fiddlehead Soup

Tara Manor Inn

10 1/2 oz. package frozen fiddlehead greens
2 cups chicken broth
2 tablespoons chopped onion
5 tablespoons butter
5 tablespoons flour
1 cup evaporated milk
salt and pepper to taste

Cook fiddleheads according to package directions. Drain, reserving liquid. Chop greens finely.

In a large saucepan bring the reserved liquid, broth and onion to a boil, reduce heat and simmer until the onion is soft. Blend together the butter and flour, forming several small balls. Drop balls into the soup, one or two at a time, and continue to cook until thickened. Stir in milk and chopped fiddleheads, season with salt and pepper. If a smoother soup is desired, purée in batches in a food processor or blender. Yields 4 servings.

Potato Cheese Soup

The Compass Rose, N.S.

2 tablespoons butter
1 cup finely chopped onion
1 cup finely chopped carrots
3 sprigs fresh parsley
2 1/2 cups chicken broth
1 1/2 - 2 cups peeled and cubed potatoes
1/2 teaspoon dry dill weed
salt and pepper to taste
1 - 1 1/2 cups grated Cheddar cheese

Melt butter in a large saucepan, add onion and carrots, cover and cook over low heat until vegetables are tender. Add the parsley, broth and potatoes. Bring to a boil, then reduce heat and simmer until potatoes are tender. Add dill and remove from heat, letting stand, covered, for 5 minutes.

Transfer soup, in batches, to a food processor or blender and process until smooth. Return to saucepan, season with salt and pepper. Gradually stir in grated cheese, bring to serving temperature but do not boil. Serve immediately. Yields 4 servings.

Creamy Clam Chowder

Shaw's Hotel

1/2 cup chopped celery
1/2 cup chopped onion
1/2 cup butter
3 tablespoons flour
2 cups milk
1/2 cup heavy cream (32% m.f.)
2 tablespoons powdered chicken stock base
2 cans clams with juice (7 oz. cans)
1 cup pre-cooked, diced potatoes
2 tablespoons chopped pimento
2 tablespoons parsley

In a large saucepan sauté the celery and onion in butter until tender. Whisk in the flour to form a roux and incorporate the milk, cream, chicken stock base and juice from the clams, stirring constantly. Add the clams, potatoes, pimento and parsley and cook over medium heat until hot and thickened. Serves 6-8.

Cream of Broccoli Soup

Shadow Lawn Country Inn

1 lb. fresh broccoli (or 2 10 oz. packages frozen broccoli)
1/4 cup finely chopped onion
2 cups chicken broth
2 tablespoons butter
1 tablespoon flour
1 teaspoon salt
pepper to taste
pinch of mace
2 cups light cream (10% m.f.)

Wash and chop broccoli, if using fresh, or thaw broccoli, if using frozen. Reserve a few pieces for a garnish, if desired. Bring broccoli, onion and chicken broth to a boil, reduce heat and simmer, covered, until tender. Cool slightly and purée in a blender or food processor in batches. In a large saucepan melt the butter, whisk in the flour, salt, pepper and mace. Slowly add the cream and stir until smooth. Add the broccoli and warm to serving temperature. Garnish with a twist of lemon or broccoli trees. For a heartier soup, omit the blender or processor step. Yields 4 servings.

Creamed Spinach Soup

Gowrie House

1 lb. spinach
4 tablespoons butter
1/4 teaspoon nutmeg
1 1/2 cups hot chicken stock
1 1/2 cups heavy cream (32% m.f.)
salt and pepper to taste
croutons

Wash and pick over spinach to remove large stems. Place spinach in a salad spinner to remove excess water and then coarsely chop.

Heat butter in a saucepan and, when bubbly, drop in spinach with nutmeg. Cook 3-4 minutes over medium heat. Chop the spinach slightly in a food processor (do not purée). Return spinach to saucepan with hot chicken stock. Add cream and heat, being careful not to boil. Season with salt and pepper and serve immediately with croutons on top. Serves 4-6.

If using canned chicken stock, use 1 cup stock plus 1/2 cup water.

Brotchan Buidhe

O'Carroll's Restaurant

1 large celery stock, chopped
1 medium onion, chopped
1 lb. carrots (5 medium), pared and chopped
salt and pepper to taste
4 cups chicken stock
2 tablespoons butter, melted
2 tablespoons flour
2 tablespoons regular oatmeal
10 oz. fresh spinach
1/4 teaspoon curry (optional)
4-6 tablespoons heavy cream (32% m.f.)

Place celery, onion, carrots, salt, pepper and chicken stock in a large stockpot and simmer 30 minutes.

Melt the butter in a small saucepan and whisk in the flour. Stir a small amount of the vegetable liquid into the flour mixture, then incorporate the roux back to the stockpot, whisking until smooth. Sprinkle the oatmeal over the soup, add the spinach which has been washed, trimmed of large stocks and stems and broken into bite-sized pieces, and curry. Simmer an additional 15 minutes and cool slightly.

Transfer the stock, in batches, to a food processor or blender and purée. Reheat before serving and spoon a tablespoon of cream into each bowl of hot soup, making a decorative swirl. Serves 4-6.

Maritime Soup Pot

Chez La Vigne

1/2 cup dry white wine
1 lb. fresh mussels, well cleaned
1/4 cup butter
1 leek (1/3 of green cut away), finely chopped
1 celery stock, finely chopped
1 large onion, finely sliced
1/2 teaspoon curry powder
3 tablespoons flour
2 3/4 cups fish stock
1 1/2 small branches fennel or 1/2 teaspoon fennel seeds
1/2 lb. fresh salmon, cut in 3/4-inch cubes
1/2 lb. fresh halibut, cut in 3/4-inch cubes
1/3 lb. fresh shrimp, peeled and deveined
10 small scallops
1 tomato, peeled, squeezed and finely chopped
1/2 cup heavy cream (32% m.f.)
1 tablespoon chopped parsley
salt and cayenne pepper to taste

Heat wine in a deep, heavy saucepan. Add mussels, cover and cook 6 minutes until shells open. Discard unopened mussels. Remove top half of shell and keep mussels warm. Reserve liquid from mussels.

Heat 1/2 of the butter in saucepan. Add leeks, celery and onion and smother until soft and glazy. Add curry and flour and mix well. Stir in fish stock and liquid from mussels. Add fennel and simmer 8 minutes. Add seafood, except mussels, and simmer for 3 minutes. Remove from heat. Without breaking fish, gently stir in tomato, cream, parsley and remaining butter in small pieces. (Chef Alex Clavel just shakes pot back and forth to blend these items.) Taste and adjust seasoning with salt and cayenne. Serve topped with mussels on the half shell. Serves 4-6.

Carrot and Zucchini Soup

The Galley Restaurant

1 1/2 teaspoons butter
1 1/2 cups seeded and chopped zucchini
1/2 cup chopped cauliflower
1/2 cup chopped carrot
1/2 cup chopped celery
1/2 cup chopped onion
1/2 teaspoon marjoram
1/4 teaspoon white pepper
1/2 cup powdered chicken stock base (2 oz.)
2 cups water
2 cups light cream (10% m.f.)

In a large pot cook all ingredients (except cream) until tender. Purée in a food processor or blender. Add 2 cups light cream and reheat gently, being careful not to boil. Serves 6.

Haitian Carrot Soup

Compass Rose, N.B.

4 cups chicken stock
1 large onion, chopped
6 medium carrots, pared and thinly sliced
generous pinch of nutmeg
2 tablespoons peanut butter
2 teaspoons Worcestershire sauce
1 large garlic clove, crushed
4 tablespoons heavy cream (32% m.f.)
sour cream and snipped chives for garnish

In a large stockpot, simmer the stock, onion, carrots, nutmeg, peanut butter, Worcestershire sauce and garlic until vegetables are tender, about 20 minutes. Cool slightly and purée in a blender or food processor until smooth. Reheat, stir in the heavy cream and serve garnished with a tablespoon of sour cream and a few snipped chives. Yields 4 servings.

Salmon Bisque

The Normaway Inn

poaching liquid*
1 lb. salmon
1/4 cup butter
1/4 cup chopped onion
1/4 cup chopped celery
3 tablespoons flour
1 teaspoon salt
1 cup light cream (10% m.f.) and 1 cup milk or 2 cups milk
1 cup tomato juice
2 tablespoons chopped fresh parsley
salt and pepper to taste

Poach salmon in poaching liquid until barely cooked. Remove salmon and cool slightly, trim skin and bones, flake meat and reserve. Reserve strained liquid.

Heat butter and sauté onion and celery over low heat for 5 minutes. Add flour and salt, stir to combine, remove from heat. Combine 1 cup of poaching liquid and milk, then gently whisk into flour mixture. Return to moderate heat and cook, stirring constantly, until smooth and thickened. Add tomato juice, parsley, seasonings and flaked salmon. Return to serving temperature, being careful not to allow bisque to boil. Serve immediately. Yields 4 servings.

Poaching Liquid
2 cups water
1/4 cup white wine
1 celery stalk with leaves, sliced
1 bay leaf
5 peppercorns

Combine all ingredients and bring to a boil.

Seafood Chowder

Zwicker's Inn

4 tablespoons butter
2 cups minced onion
1 1/2 teaspoons salt
2 1/2 teaspoons thyme
1 tablespoon celery salt
1/8 teaspoon pepper
2 cups cubed potatoes (medium-sized cubes)
2 cups heavy cream (32% m.f.)
2/3 lb. halibut or other white fish
1/3 lb. scallops, cut in chowder-sized pieces
3/4 cup sour cream
1 1/2 cups milk, if using halibut, or 1 1/3 cups milk for other fish
1/4 lb. cooked lobster meat and juice, in bite-sized pieces

Sauté onion in butter only until the raw onion odour is gone. Stir in salt, thyme, celery salt and pepper and reserve. Over low heat, boil potato cubes in water until tender. Drain and add to onions.

Poach halibut in heavy cream until barely cooked. Remove with slotted spoon, break into chowder-sized pieces and add to onion mixture. Poach scallops in the same cream. Bring to a gentle boil, remove from heat and let stand 5 minutes.

Gently stir sour cream, milk, lobster meat and juice, scallops and cream into onion mixture. Reheat until hot but not boiling and serve. This chowder's flavour is enhanced by refrigerating overnight and serving the following day. Serves 6-8.

Cream of Herb Soup

The Garden Restaurant

3 cups beef or chicken stock
3 handfuls of assorted spring herbs (i.e. chervil, parsley, chives, basil, sorrel), coarsely chopped
3/4 tablespoon flour
1 1/2 tablespoons butter
6 egg yolks
1 1/2 cups heavy cream (32% m.f.)
salt, pepper and nutmeg to taste
seasoned croutons

Bring stock to a boil, add herbs, lower heat and simmer for a few minutes. Knead together the flour and butter, forming into small balls. Add to boiling stock, one or two at a time, stirring constantly until thickened. In a small bowl mix together the yolks and cream. Stir a little of the hot stock into the egg mixture, then return to the broth and bring back to serving temperature. Be very careful not to boil. Serve topped with seasoned croutons.

Seasoned Croutons
4 slices white bread
2 tablespoons butter
1 small garlic clove, minced (optional)

Cut bread into small cubes. Melt butter in a skillet and sauté garlic, if using, for 1-2 minutes. Add bread cubes, sauté over medium heat, stirring and tossing the cubes until golden brown. Transfer croutons to paper towels and cool.

Salads

Poppy Seed Dressing

The Garrison House Inn

1 small egg
1 tablespoon granulated sugar
1 1/2 teaspoons Dijon-style mustard
1/3 cup red wine vinegar
pinch of salt
1 tablespoon finely chopped onion
1/2 cup olive oil
1/2 cup vegetable oil
2 tablespoons poppy seeds

Combine egg, sugar, mustard, vinegar, salt and onion in a food processor or blender. Process one minute. Add oils in a slow stream, processing only until blended. Stir in poppy seeds. Refrigerate and serve with spinach or other salad greens. Yields 1 1/2 cups dressing.

Rossmount Pink Radish House Dressing

The Rossmount Inn

3/4 cup quartered radishes
1 clove garlic
1 tablespoon white vinegar
1 tablespoon wine vinegar
3 tablespoons sour cream
1 cup egg-based mayonnaise (good quality)

Clean, trim and quarter radishes and garlic. Process radishes, garlic and vinegars in a food processor until fine. Whisk sour cream and mayonnaise into radish mixture until well blended. Refrigerate to blend flavours. Yields 2 cups dressing.

Herb and Garlic Salad Dressing

Zwicker's Inn

2 teaspoons chopped green onion
2 tablespoons chopped fresh parsley
2 teaspoons sugar
2 teaspoons Dijon mustard
4 tablespoons lemon juice, freshly squeezed
3/4 teaspoon salt
1 teaspoon crushed tarragon
1/2 teaspoon pepper
1/2 cup wine vinegar
2 garlic cloves, crushed
1 1/3 cups olive oil

Combine all ingredients in a blender or food processor and blend until smooth. Yields 2 cups dressing.

Tarragon Dressing

Benoit's Restaurant

2 teaspoons Dijon-style mustard
1 egg yolk
1/2 teaspoon dried tarragon
1 1/2 teaspoons dried savory
salt and pepper to taste
2 tablespoons finely chopped onion
1 large or 2 small garlic cloves, minced
1 1/4 cups olive oil
1/3 cup wine vinegar

Place mustard and egg yolk in a food processor or blender and combine well. Add seasonings, onion and garlic and process. Slowly add olive oil in a steady stream until emulsified. Add wine vinegar, combine well and refrigerate. Yields 2 cups dressing.

Tomato Salad Provençale

The Algonquin

4-6 firm tomatoes
1 English cucumber
2 shallots
5-6 fresh basil leaves or 1 teaspoon dry
1 cup vegetable oil
1 cup vinegar
chives to garnish

Core tomatoes and place on cutting board, cored side down. Cut tomatoes as if making wedges but stop a half inch before cutting through. Place tomatoes in a shallow glass dish and reserve in refrigerator.

Dice cucumber and peeled shallots very finely. Chop basil. Combine cucumber, shallots, basil, oil and vinegar and mix well. Pour marinade over tomatoes, cover and refrigerate 6-8 hours. To serve, place tomatoes on salad plates, spread wedges in flower fashion. Whisk marinade and ladle a small amount over tomatoes. Garnish with chives. Serves 4-6.

Waldorf Salad with Honey Lemon Dressing

The Maple Inn

1/2 cup lemon juice
1/2 cup vegetable oil
1 teaspoon salt
1/2 teaspoon white pepper
2 tablespoons sugar
2 tablespoons honey
2 cups unpeeled, diced apple
1 cup thinly sliced celery
1/2 cup chopped walnuts
1/2 cup seedless raisins
2 tablespoons chopped green onion
lettuce leaves

Combine lemon juice, oil, salt, pepper, sugar and honey and

beat well to emulsify.

Dice apples and toss with salad dressing immediately to prevent browning. Add celery, nuts, raisins and onion. Toss lightly and refrigerate. When ready to serve arrange apple mixture over lettuce leaves with a slotted spoon. Serves 4-6.

Caesar Salad

The Inn at Bay Fortune

romaine lettuce to serve 4
1-2 garlic cloves
3-4 anchovy fillets, drained
2-4 drops Tabasco sauce
several drops Worcestershire sauce
1/2 tablespoon Dijon-style mustard
yolk of 1 small egg
1/4 cup olive oil
juice of 1/2 lemon
1/4 cup freshly grated Parmesan cheese
croutons

Wash and dry lettuce and tear into bite-sized pieces. Set aside. In a large wooden salad bowl crush together the garlic and anchovies. Stir in the Tabasco and Worcestershire sauces. Mix in the mustard, egg yolk, olive oil and lemon juice, stirring until well incorporated and slightly thickened. Toss the lettuce and Parmesan with dressing and add croutons. Serves 4.

Greek Salad

Shaw's Hotel

romaine lettuce to serve 4
1 purple onion, cut in rings
tomato wedges
Greek olives
cucumber, peeled, cut lengthwise, seeded and sliced into sticks
1/4 lb. feta cheese, crumbled

Dressing
1 cup egg-based mayonnaise
1 clove garlic, crushed
3 tablespoons raspberry vinegar
1 teaspoon chopped fresh thyme or 1/4 teaspoon dry
1 teaspoon chopped fresh oregano or 1/4 teaspoon dry
1/2 teaspoon Worcestershire sauce

Combine dressing ingredients in a blender or food processor. Chill until ready to serve. To assemble, arrange prepared romaine, onion rings, tomato wedges, olives, cucumber pieces and crumbled cheese on 4 chilled salad plates. Top with dressing. Serves 4.

Marinated Mushroom Artichoke Salad

The Gowrie House

1 small egg (or 1/2 large egg), beaten
1 tablespoon tarragon vinegar
1 tablespoon lemon juice
1 1/2 teaspoons Worcestershire sauce
1 small clove garlic, crushed
1/8 teaspoon dry mustard
1/4 teaspoon black pepper
1/4 teaspoon white pepper
1/2 teaspoon salt
1/3 cup olive oil
3/4 lb. fresh white mushrooms, sliced
1 14 oz. can artichoke hearts, drained and quartered
Boston or Bibb lettuce leaves
fresh chives, parsley or basil as garnish

Combine first 9 ingredients and beat well. Slowly add olive oil while stirring with a whisk until oil is well combined. Add mushrooms and artichokes to the marinade, stir to coat, cover and let stand at room temperature for up to 8 hours, stirring occasionally.

To serve, remove artichokes and mushrooms with a slotted spoon and arrange on lettuce-lined plates. Garnish with fresh herbs. Serves 4-6.

Captain's House Caesar Salad

The Captain's House

2 egg yolks
2 tablespoons olive oil
1 tablespoon wine vinegar
pinch of dry mustard
romaine lettuce, head lettuce and spinach to serve 6
4 slices crispy bacon, crumbled
1/4 cup crumbled blue cheese
2-4 anchovy fillets, drained and chopped
dash of fresh lemon juice

Whisk together the egg, oil, vinegar and mustard. Prepare lettuces and spinach. Toss greens with dressing. Top with bacon, cheese and anchovies. Toss lightly and add a dash of lemon juice. Serves 4-6.

Cooper's Inn Waldorf Salad

Cooper's Inn

1/2 cup diced celery
2 teaspoons minced green onion
2 tart Granny Smith apples, peeled and thinly sliced
1/2 cup walnut halves
2 oz. blue cheese, crumbled
1/2 cup egg-based mayonnaise
1/2 cup crème fraîche (or sour cream or unflavoured yogurt)
4 large leaves radicchio plus other assorted lettuces

In a medium bowl combine the celery, onions, apples, walnut halves and crumbled cheese. Whisk together the mayonnaise and crème fraîche. Add to the bowl and toss gently to mix. To serve, place a radicchio leaf in the centre of 4 serving plates and place the other lettuce leaves around it. Top with the salad mixture. Yields 4 servings.

Salad Niçoise

The Galley

1 head romaine lettuce, torn in bite-sized pieces
6 1/2 oz. tin chunk tuna, drained
1/2 lb. fresh green beans, cooked and halved
4 hard-boiled eggs
2 potatoes, boiled, cooled and sliced
black olives

Salad Dressing
1/2 cup red wine vinegar
2 garlic cloves, crushed
1 tablespoon Dijon-style mustard
1 teaspoon salt
1/2 teaspoon oregano
1 teaspoon fresh basil or 1/4 teaspoon dry
1/2 cup oil
pepper and lemon juice to taste

To make dressing, whisk together ingredients until well blended. Refrigerate. Combine salad ingredients in a large salad bowl. Pour dressing over salad and gently toss to coat. Serve on individual plates. Serves 4.

Carrot Salad

Heron Country Inn

2 lbs. carrots
2 green peppers, thinly sliced
2 onions, thinly sliced
1 cup sugar (scant)
1/2 cup vegetable oil
3/4 cup white vinegar
1 10 oz. can tomato soup
salt and pepper to taste

Pare and slice the carrots in rounds. Cook 10 minutes until barely tender. Drain and cool quickly with cold running water. Place in a large bowl. Thinly slice the peppers and onions and add to the carrots.

In a small saucepan combine the sugar, oil, vinegar and tomato soup. Bring to a boil and pour over the vegetables. Season with salt and pepper. Store covered in the refrigerator up to 2 weeks, stirring occasionally.

Meats and Poultry

Beef Wellington

Shadow Lawn Country Inn

1 whole beef tenderloin fillet, 2-3 lbs.
2 tablespoons butter
1/2 onion, finely chopped
1 cup chopped fresh mushrooms
1/2 lb. liver pâté
1 1/2 cups flour
1/2 teaspoon salt
1 tablespoon minced parsley
1 teaspoon celery seeds
2/3 cup shortening or lard
4-5 tablespoons ice water
1 egg yolk plus 1 tablespoon water

Early in the day cook the tenderloin in a preheated 325°F oven to rare, 23-25 minutes per pound. Cool, then refrigerate.

Prepare duxelles by sautéing onions and mushrooms in butter until tender. Drain on a paper towel. Mix together with pâté and spread over top and sides of tenderloin.

Prepare pastry by combining flour, salt, parsley and celery seeds and then cutting in shortening with a pastry blender. Bind with cold water and roll out to a rectangle. Place fillet on pastry, coated side down. Fold pastry and pinch together. Place seam side down on a greased baking dish. Brush with egg wash (1 egg yolk beaten together with 1 tablespoon water). Prick with a fork several times and bake in a preheated 400°F oven, 35-40 minutes for rare, 50-60 minutes for medium to well done. Let stand 10 minutes before serving. Yields 6 servings.

Hungarian Goulash

New Consulate Restaurant

1 onion
1 green pepper
3/4 lb. fresh tomatoes (2 large)
2 tablespoons flour
1 teaspoon salt
1/4 teaspoon pepper
1 1/2 lbs. good quality beefsteak, cut in 1-inch cubes
2 tablespoons butter
1 tablespoon tomato paste
1 tablespoon sweet paprika
1 teaspoon sugar
1 bay leaf
1/4 teaspoon nutmeg
1 beef bouillon cube
1 1/2 cups boiling water
1 cup sour cream
fresh parsley to garnish

Dice onion and green pepper. Peel and coarsely chop tomatoes. Combine flour, salt and pepper and coat cubed beef with flour mixture.

Melt butter in a heavy-bottomed saucepan. Sauté onions in butter for 2 minutes until softened. Raise heat and quickly brown seasoned beef cubes in saucepan with onions. Add green pepper, tomatoes, tomato paste, sweet paprika, sugar, bay leaf and nutmeg to beef mixture. Dissolve bouillon cube in boiling water and add to saucepan. Bring to boil, reduce heat and simmer 30 minutes.

Fold sour cream into goulash, garnish with fresh parsley and serve over hot buttered noodles. Serves 4-6.

Beef Bourgignon

Boscawen Inn

1 1/2 lbs. lean beef, cut in 1-inch cubes
flour, salt and pepper for dredging
1 oz. salt pork, diced
1 tablespoon vegetable oil
1/2 teaspoon salt
pinch of pepper
pinch of thyme
1/2 cup Burgundy wine
2 - 2 1/2 cups beef stock or broth
1 small garlic clove, minced
1/2 small onion, sliced
1 small bouquet garni
4 oz. fresh mushrooms
1 tablespoon butter
3/4 teaspoon lemon juice
12-16 small white onions, peeled
1 tablespoon butter
1 tablespoon water
1 tablespoon sugar
fresh parsley sprigs for garnish

Cut beef in cubes, dredge in seasoned flour and set aside. Cover diced pork with water and boil 2-3 minutes, drain. Place pork in a large saucepan, sauté over medium heat until lightly browned, remove from pan and reserve. Add oil to the saucepan and brown beef cubes on all sides. Season with salt, pepper and thyme. Add wine, beef stock, garlic, onion slices and bouquet garni to saucepan and simmer 1 1/2 - 2 hours, until meat is tender.

In the meantime, sauté mushrooms in butter and lemon juice until browned and set aside. In a clean saucepan glaze whole onions in butter, 1 tablespoon water and sugar until browned.

Place mushrooms, pork scraps, glazed onions in pan with beef and cook an additional 15 minutes. Thicken sauce with a little flour and cold water, if desired. Remove bouquet garni and serve with a sprinkling of fresh parsley as garnish. Serves 4.

Bouquet Garni
Tie together a combination of herbs, such as a bay leaf, a sprig of parsley, basil, thyme, etc., in a cheesecloth.

Grilled Fillets of Beef with Mushroom Sauce

Victoria's Village Inn

4-6 fillets of beef
1/4 cup butter, melted
pinch of white pepper
1/2 teaspoon salt
6 tablespoons flour
1/2 cup light cream (10% m.f.)
10 1/2 oz. can condensed beef broth
3/4 cup water
2 tablespoons sweet vermouth
12 large mushrooms, sliced

Grill fillets to desired degree of doneness. In the meantime melt butter over medium heat, stir in the pepper, salt and flour. Stir gently over low heat for 5 minutes but do not let brown. Whisk in the cream, broth, water and vermouth. Continue cooking and stirring until sauce thickens and bubbles. Add the mushrooms and cook 5 minutes. Serve warm over steaks. Yields 3 cups sauce.

Gingered Leg of Lamb

The Normaway Inn

1 leg of lamb, 4-6 lbs.
2 teaspoons grated fresh ginger root
2 tablespoons vegetable oil
2 teaspoons lemon zest (grated peel)
juice of 1 lemon
1/2 teaspoon paprika
salt and pepper to taste
6 garlic slivers

Trim lamb of fat. Combine ginger, oil, lemon zest and juice, paprika, salt and pepper and blend well. With a sharp knife puncture lamb and insert garlic slivers. Brush with oil mixture and let stand 1-2 hours at room temperature.

Preheat oven to 500°F and sear lamb for 10 minutes. Reduce heat to 325°F and continue baking until roast reaches desired internal temperature on a meat thermometer (145°F rare, 155°F medium, 175°F well done), approximately 15-18 minutes per pound. Baste lamb with pan drippings and marinade during cooking time. Make gravy with remaining pan drippings. Serves 6-8.

Butterflied Leg of Lamb

Gowrie House

1 leg of lamb, deboned
3/4 cup soya sauce
3/4 cup corn oil
4 onions, chopped coarsely
1 teaspoon ground cumin
1 teaspoon ground coriander
1 teaspoon curry powder
1 teaspoon ground cardamom

Trim lamb of all excess fat and sinew. Combine remaining ingredients and mix well. Place lamb in a large shallow dish and pour marinade over, turning lamb to coat. Cover and marinate 12-24 hours in refrigerator. Turn meat 2-4 times while marinating.

Place lamb on a broiler pan and pat with onions from the marinade. Broil 10 inches from heat 15-20 minutes, turn lamb, baste with sauce and pat more onions over leg. Broil 15-20 minutes longer until internal temperature reaches 145-155°F or until meat is well browned on outside but pink inside. Serves 6-8.

Ham Croquettes Bayonne

O'Carroll's Restaurant

3 tablespoons butter
1/3 cup flour
1 cup milk
2 1/2 cups finely chopped cooked ham
1 tablespoon finely chopped chives
egg wash (beaten egg yolk and 1 tablespoon water)
dry bread crumbs
vegetable oil for frying
1 large onion, sliced in rings and sautéed in butter (optional)

Melt butter in a saucepan, blend in flour and cook for one minute. Gradually whisk milk into mixture until smooth. Cook over medium heat until thickened. Remove from heat and stir in ham and chives. Spread mixture in a pie plate, cover and refrigerate until well chilled.

When mixture is cold, shape into croquettes that are no larger than 1 x 1 x 2 1/2 inches. Dip croquettes into egg wash and then roll in crumbs. Dry on a wire rack for up to one hour and then deep fry in 375°F vegetable oil, a few at a time, for 2-4 minutes until golden. Drain on paper towels. Serve hot, garnished with onion rings which have been sautéed in butter, if desired.

Savory Pork Tenderloin with Red Currant Sauce

The Galley

2 large pork tenderloins (1 1/2 lbs. total)
1 cup bread crumbs
1/4 cup pared and chopped apple
1/4 cup chopped onion
1/4 cup chopped celery
2 teaspoons dried summer savory
2 tablespoons white wine
1 egg, beaten
salt and pepper to taste
1 cup dry breadcrumbs
2 tablespoons vegetable oil

Sauce
1/4 cup red currant jelly
1 teaspoon chicken stock
2 tablespoons white wine

Remove all fat and tissue from the pork tenderloins. Slice almost in half horizontally and lay out flat. Pound between sheets of waxed paper with a meat mallet to 1/2-inch thickness.

Prepare dressing by combining crumbs, apple, onion, celery, savory and wine. Stir in 1 tablespoon of the beaten egg to bind and season with salt and pepper. Divide the dressing between the tenderloins and roll up jelly-roll fashion. Dip in the remaining egg, then in the dry bread crumbs. Brown on all sides in hot oil; transfer to an ovenproof dish and bake in a preheated 375°F oven until no longer pink, about 20-25 minutes.

Prepare sauce by combining jelly, stock and wine in a small saucepan over medium heat. To serve, arrange slices of stuffed tenderloin on warm plates, and top with warm sauce. Serves 4.

Pork Tenderloin with Stilton Crust

The Garden Restaurant

1 1/2 lbs. pork tenderloin, cut in 1/2" medallions
salt and pepper to taste
flour for dusting
1 tablespoon butter
1 1/2 cups beef broth or medium dry white wine
3 tablespoons flour
2 tablespoons butter
3 oz. Stilton or other blue cheese
1-2 tablespoons bread crumbs
1 tablespoon chopped fresh parsley

Flatten pork medallions slightly, season with salt and pepper and dust with flour. Sauté in melted butter to desired doneness, turning once. Transfer meat to a platter, keep warm.

Deglaze pan with broth or wine. Mix together 3 tablespoons flour and 2 tablespoons butter, forming several small balls. Add to stock, one at a time, until desired thickness is achieved. In the meantime, blend together the cheese and crumbs, spoon a small amount on top of each medallion and broil until bubbly. Serve topped with sauce and parsley. Yields 4 servings.

Recipe was tested using 1 cup stock and 1/2 cup wine.

Swiss Pork Chops

Milford House

4 medium-sized pork chops
1/3 cup flour
1/3 cup milk
1 egg
dry bread crumbs seasoned with salt and pepper
2 tablespoons vegetable oil
4 small slices cooked ham
4 slices Swiss cheese

Coat the chops with flour, shaking off excess. Whisk together the milk and egg. Dip the chops into egg-milk mixture, then in seasoned bread crumbs, coating evenly.

Heat oil in a sauté skillet, brown chops on both sides, remove to ovenproof baking dish. Bake chops in preheated 375°F oven until no longer pink inside, 15-20 minutes, depending upon thickness. Cover each chop with a slice of ham and a slice of cheese. Return to oven and bake long enough for the cheese to melt. Serves 4.

Braised Pork Chops with Wild Blueberry Sauce

The Maple Inn

2 tablespoons vegetable oil
2 tablespoons butter
4-6 boneless pork loin chops
1 teaspoon minced garlic
1/2 teaspoon minced fresh sage or pinch of dry
1 cup chicken stock
1 cup dry white wine
3/4 cup fresh or frozen wild blueberries

Melt oil and butter together in a heavy skillet. Sauté pork until golden brown on both sides. Add garlic, sage, chicken stock, wine and blueberries. Reduce heat and simmer until pork is just cooked.

With a slotted spoon remove chops and blueberries to serving dish. Place sauce in a small pitcher and pour desired amount over chops. Serve with steamed rice, garnished with fresh sage. Serves 4-6.

Roast Loin of Pork with Maple Glaze

Tara Manor Inn

3 1/2 - 4 lb. boneless loin of pork
1/2 cup maple syrup
1/2 cup liquid honey
1 cup dry ginger ale
2 cloves garlic, crushed
1/2 teaspoon salt
2 cups apple juice
3 tablespoons cornstarch mixed with cold water (optional)

Preheat oven to 375°F. Place roast, fat side up, in a roasting pan. Mix together the maple syrup, honey, ginger ale, garlic and salt; pour over roast. Bake 15 minutes, then reduce heat to 325°F and continue to bake for 1 1/4 - 1 1/2 hours, basting occasionally, until a meat thermometer inserted into the centre of the roast registers 170°F.

Transfer meat to a warm platter and tent with aluminum foil. Deglaze pan with apple juice. Thicken gravy with 3 tablespoons cornstarch mixed with cold water, if desired. Serve sliced and topped with a little pan gravy. Serves 6-8.

Veal Scalloppine à la Crème

Benoit's Restaurant

1 - 1 1/2 lbs. veal cutlets
white flour for dredging
salt and pepper
1 tablespoon butter
1 tablespoon oil
2 tablespoons chopped shallots
1/4 cup white wine
1 cup heavy cream (32% m.f.)

Prepare veal cutlets by removing membrane and pounding between waxed paper until very thin. Dredge cutlets in flour, salt and pepper and reserve. Add butter and oil to a skillet and heat to very hot. Quickly add cutlets and cook until golden brown, turning once. Remove and keep warm.

Pour off excess oil from skillet, add shallots and deglaze pan with white wine. Add cream and simmer for 4 minutes until sauce is slightly thickened. Add cutlets to sauce and serve immediately on a bed of pasta. Serves 4.

Veal with Gruyère and Mustard Sauce

Cooper's Inn

1 1/2 lbs. veal cutlets, well trimmed and sliced into medallions
2 tablespoons olive oil
1 tablespoon butter
2 cloves garlic, crushed
3/4 cup dry white wine
7 oz. Gruyère cheese, cubed
several drops of brandy
1 cup flour
2 eggs, beaten
1 cup dry bread crumbs
2 tablespoons olive oil
1 tablespoon minced green onion
3/4 cup dry white wine
1 tablespoon Dijon-style mustard
3 tablespoons butter

Sauté prepared veal medallions in hot oil and butter until mostly cooked and browned on both sides. Remove from pan, drain on paper towels and refrigerate until cold.

In a medium saucepan, heat the garlic and wine. Add cheese and stir until thoroughly blended. Add a few drops of brandy to taste. Dip the cold medallions into the warm cheese mixture, then into the flour, egg and breadcrumbs, in that order.

Sauté coated medallions in oil until golden and heated through. Remove to a warm serving platter. Deglaze the pan by adding the onions, wine, mustard and butter. Quickly reduce by half and pour over medallions. Serves 4.

Veal with Tarragon

The Captain's House

4 veal cutlets, about 6-8 oz. each
2 tablespoons butter
1/2 cup sliced mushrooms
shallot mix
1/4 cup dry sherry
1/2 cup brown sauce
pinch of dry tarragon
1/4 cup heavy cream (32% m.f.)
salt and pepper to taste

Pound cutlets to 1/8-inch thickness between two pieces of waxed paper. Brown lightly in butter. Add mushrooms and 2 tablespoons shallot mix, sauté gently and add sherry, brown sauce, tarragon and heavy cream. Simmer gently and season with salt and pepper. Serves 4.

Shallot Mix
Place 1 red onion and 1 white onion in a blender. Add enough white wine to blender to form a smooth purée.

Brown Sauce
1 1/2 tablespoons butter
1/2 small onion, chopped
1/2 cup dry red wine
3/4 cup beef broth
1/2 bay leaf
1/2 teaspoon parsley
1 tablespoon butter
1 1/2 tablespoons flour

Melt butter in a saucepan and add onion. Cook until onion turns golden brown, add wine and broth and bring to a boil. Add bay leaf and parsley and boil briskly until liquid is reduced by a third.

Knead together butter and flour. Form into small balls and add to boiling sauce, one at a time, stirring constantly, until sauce reaches the consistency of heavy cream.

Scalloppine Di Vitello Alla Piemontese (Veal in Tomato Wine Sauce)

La Perla

1 1/4 lbs. veal cutlets, trimmed
flour for dusting
2 eggs, beaten
2 teaspoons grated Parmesan cheese
2 teaspoons dried parsley
1 1/2 cups dry bread crumbs
1/2 cup oil

Sauce
2 teaspoons butter
1/2 cup chopped onion
2 teaspoons fresh basil or 1/2 teaspoon dry
1 cup chopped tomatoes
salt and pepper to taste
1/2 cup dry white wine
2 tablespoons brandy
1 teaspoon sugar
1 cup heavy cream (32% m.f.)

Trim cutlets, dust with flour. Beat eggs, add cheese and parsley. Dip cutlets in egg mixture, then in bread crumbs. Heat the oil in a sauté pan and brown, turning once. Remove and keep warm.

To make sauce, melt the butter in a skillet, add onion and sauté until golden, add basil and tomatoes and cook 1 minute. Add salt, pepper, wine and brandy and cook until reduced by a half. Stir in sugar and cream and thicken. Pour sauce in a serving dish and lay veal on top. Serve with buttered fettucine. Serves 4.

Chicken Breasts in Maple Cream Sauce

The Maple Inn

4 boneless chicken breasts
1 tablespoon butter
1 tablespoon vegetable oil
1/2 cup pure maple syrup
1 cup heavy cream (32% m.f.)

Sauté chicken in a saucepan in the butter and oil, turning frequently to avoid overbrowning. Remove chicken from pan and keep warm on a platter.

Deglaze the pan with a little water, add maple syrup and reduce over medium heat until slightly thickened, about 4 minutes. Stir in the cream and simmer, stirring constantly, until sauce is thickened and coats a spoon. Return chicken to sauce to warm through and serve on a bed of rice. Serves 4.

Chicken Cassis

The Compass Rose, N. S.

4 boneless chicken breasts
flour for dredging
2 tablespoons butter
2 cloves garlic, minced
1 tablespoon butter
4 tablespoons Crème de Cassis liqueur
2 tablespoons currant jelly, melted
2 tablespoons vodka
2 tablespoons heavy cream (32% m.f.)
2 teaspoons black currants

Rinse and pat dry chicken. Dredge in flour and sauté with garlic in butter until golden brown. Remove from pan and keep warm. Add remaining butter to the sauté pan, then stir in the Crème de Cassis, jelly, vodka and heavy cream. Reduce over medium heat, stirring constantly until slightly thickened. Add currants and spoon over warm chicken breasts. Serves 4.

Chicken Marquis

The Amherst Shore Country Inn

4 chicken breasts, deboned
salt and pepper to taste
2 cloves garlic, minced
2 cups blanched spinach
4 1/2 oz. (128 g) Camembert or Brie cheese
4 slices bacon, partially cooked
1/4 cup butter, melted

Remove all fat from chicken breasts, rinse and pat dry. Place breasts between two sheets of waxed paper and pound with a meat mallet until they are slightly flattened and of a uniform thickness.

Sprinkle chicken with salt and pepper. Spread 1/4 of the garlic on each breast, top with 1/2 cup of spinach and 1/4 of the cheese round which has been cut in 4-5 pieces. Roll up chicken breast and wrap with bacon. Place seam side down in a shallow casserole. Brush chicken with melted butter and bake in a preheated 350°F oven for 35-45 minutes until done. Baste frequently with melted butter and pan juices during cooking. Yields 4 servings.

Chicken Manor Inn

The Manor Inn

4-6 boneless chicken breasts
4-6 slices mozzarella cheese
3 tablespoons garlic butter
flour
egg wash (1 egg beaten with 2 tablespoons water)
fresh bread crumbs
2-4 tablespoons butter

Trim chicken breasts of fat and membrane. Place each breast, smooth side down, between two pieces of waxed paper and pound with a meat mallet until thin. Place a cheese slice and 1 1/2 teaspoons of garlic butter in centre of each breast, fold and press edges to seal.

Roll each breast in flour, dip in egg wash and roll in bread crumbs.

In a skillet, melt butter and sauté breasts for 2 minutes on each side. Preheat oven to 400°F. Arrange breasts in a shallow casserole being careful not to overlap. Bake 5-10 minutes. To test for doneness, squeeze down on chicken. If cheese oozes, chicken is cooked. Yields 4-6 servings.

Garlic Butter
2-3 cloves garlic
1/4 cup butter

Boil garlic cloves in water in a small saucepan for 5 minutes. Drain. Crush garlic and mix well with softened butter. Makes 1/4 cup or 4 tablespoons garlic butter.

Spicy Szechwan Pecan Chicken

Silver Spoon Restaurant

1 teaspoon celery salt
1 teaspoon cayenne pepper
1 teaspoon white pepper
1 teaspoon dry mustard
1 teaspoon fennel seeds
1 teaspoon paprika
1 teaspoon oregano
1 teaspoon ground sage
1 teaspoon ground thyme
1 teaspoon ground coriander
1 teaspoon finely chopped onion
1 teaspoon finely chopped garlic
6 boneless chicken breasts
1 cup chicken stock
1 cup white wine
1 shallot, chopped
1 1/2 teaspoons heavy cream
1 teaspoon Szechwan peppercorns, toasted and crushed
1/2 cup unsalted butter
1/2 teaspoon minced garlic
2 tablespoons butter
1 tablespoon oil
1 teaspoon chopped fresh parsley
1/2 cup pecans, toasted
1 mango

Combine first 12 ingredients and mix well. Coat uncooked chicken breasts with spice mixture. Place breasts in a single layer on a cookie sheet and set aside.

Combine chicken stock, wine, shallot, cream and peppercorns in a saucepan. Bring to a boil and reduce by one half. Whisk cold, unsalted butter, a tablespoon at a time, into sauce. Add garlic and keep sauce warm.

In a skillet heat 2 tablespoons butter and oil over medium heat. Sauté breasts, in two batches if necessary, about 4-5 minutes per side or until no longer pink inside. Add parsley and pecans to sauce. Arrange sautéed breasts on plates, pour sauce over and arrange sliced mango on breasts. Serves 4-6.

Szechwan peppercorns, also known as Hong Kong or Chinese peppercorns, are light brown in colour and available in Chinese specialty stores.

Chicken Pesto

Tattingstone Inn

6 6 oz. deboned chicken breasts
1 1/2 cups cooked spinach
2 cloves garlic, minced
1 1/2 cups cooked wild rice
2 tablespoons pesto sauce*

Spread out chicken breasts but do not pound to flatten. Lightly combine spinach, garlic, rice and pesto sauce. Divide spinach mixture into 6 portions and place one portion on each breast. Fold breasts to encase filling and place, seam side down, on a lightly greased shallow dish. Bake uncovered in a preheated 350°F oven for 30-35 minutes until done. Serve immediately. Yields 6 servings.

Pesto Sauce
In a food processor combine equal amounts of chopped fresh basil, peanut oil and Parmesan cheese. Process until smooth. Stores indefinitely in a refrigerator.

Chicken Milanese

The Dundee Arms Inn

4 chicken breasts, deboned and skinned
1/2 cup flour
1 egg, beaten
1 1/2 cups dry bread crumbs
3 tablespoons vegetable oil
1/2 lb. sliced fresh mushrooms
salt and pepper to taste
4 oz. Swiss cheese, thinly sliced

Rinse and pat dry chicken breasts. Coat with flour, then dip in the beaten egg. Roll in bread crumbs being careful to cover the entire breast. Refrigerate 20 minutes.

Heat the oil in a large sauté pan on high until it begins to smoke. Quickly brown the chicken, turning once, for approximately 8 minutes or until the chicken is no longer pink inside. During the last 5 minutes of cooking, add the mushrooms to the pan.

Quickly remove the cooked breasts and mushrooms to an ovenproof serving platter. Season with salt and pepper. Layer the sliced cheese over the chicken and broil until bubbly and hot. Serves 4.

Chicken Elizabeth

Blomidon Inn

4 boneless chicken breasts
salt and pepper to taste
4 oz. crab (4 1/2 oz. tin, well drained)
1 cup spinach, coarsely chopped
2 oz. Swiss cheese, in small cubes
puff pastry, rolled 1/8-inch thick, 3 x 5 inches
egg wash (1 egg yolk beaten with 1 tablespoon water)
hollandaise sauce

Flatten chicken breasts with a meat mallet between waxed paper. Season lightly with salt and pepper. Arrange a quarter of the crab, spinach and cheese on each of the chicken breasts. Fold chicken breast around filling. Place stuffed chicken breasts on pastry rectangles. Fold pastry around chicken, tucking in edges and sealing on bottom to totally enclose meat. Arrange breasts, seam side down, in shallow baking dish.

Brush pastry with egg wash and bake in a preheated 400°F oven for 20 minutes. Serve with hollandaise sauce. Yields 4 servings.

Hollandaise Sauce
3 egg yolks
1 tablespoon cold water
1/4 teaspoon salt
pinch pepper
1 tablespoon lemon juice
1/4 cup butter, melted
1 teaspoon Dijon-style mustard (optional)

In top of a double boiler, beat egg yolks, water, salt and pepper with a wire whisk until thick. Set over hot (not boiling) water. Gradually add the lemon juice while beating constantly. Continue to beat and cook until the sauce is the consistency of thick cream. Remove the double boiler from heat, leaving top in place. Slowly beat melted butter into sauce and continue to mix until it is thoroughly blended. Add Dijon mustard, if desired. Yields 1/2 cups.

Turkey Divan

Rossmount Inn

1 bunch fresh broccoli or 10 oz. package frozen
1 1/2 cups cooked, cubed turkey
1 can cream of chicken soup
1/2 cup egg-based mayonnaise (good quality)
1/2 teaspoon lemon juice
1/4 teaspoon curry powder
1/4 cup sharp cheese, shredded
1/2 cup toasted bread crumbs
1 tablespoon butter

Cook broccoli until barely tender and cut into bite-sized pieces. In a two-quart casserole layer turkey and broccoli.

Combine soup, mayonnaise, lemon juice, curry and cheese, mixing well. Pour over turkey mixture. Top with bread crumbs and dot with butter. Bake in a preheated 350°F oven for 25-30 minutes until browned and bubbly. Serves 4.

Cornish Game Hens with Wild Rice Dressing

Amherst Shore Country Inn

1 1/2 cups wild rice, rinsed
3 cups boiling water
1/2 teaspoon salt
6 tablespoons long-grain white rice
1 cup chicken stock
1 cup fresh cranberries, sliced
2 tablespoons white sugar
1 tablespoon Grand Marnier liqueur
2 tablespoons orange juice
2 tablespoons coarsely grated orange peel
4 Cornish game hens, about 1 lb. each
1/2 teaspoon salt
1/2 cup melted butter
1/2 cup orange juice

Cook the wild rice in a large saucepan with the boiling water and salt for approximately one hour. Add additional water if necessary. Drain, rinse and set aside. Prepare long-grain rice by simmering in chicken stock for 20-25 minutes. Combine with wild rice in a large bowl and cool. Stir in sliced cranberries, sugar, Grand Marnier, orange juice and orange peel.

Wash the game hens both inside and out and pat dry. Sprinkle a little salt in the cavity of each hen. Divide the dressing among the birds and stuff lightly, closing them with a small skewer. Place the birds in a foil-lined baking dish. Generously baste with the melted butter and orange juice. Cover loosely with foil and bake in a 350°F oven for half an hour. Remove foil and continue to bake 1 - 1 1/4 hours, basting frequently, until hens are tender and brown. Serves 4.

Medallions of Tenderloin à L'Homard

Upper Deck

4 servings of beef tenderloin
8 oz. cooked lobster meat
2 tablespoons butter
2 cups Hollandaise sauce

Cook the tenderloins in butter to your liking over medium heat. Add lobster to the warmed Hollandaise sauce and spread on top of tenderloins. (Serves 4)

Hollandaise Sauce
1 cup butter, clarified
3 egg yolks
1/4 cup white wine
1/4 cup lemon juice
1/2 teaspoon Tabasco sauce
pinch of salt and pepper

Clarify butter by melting and skimming off foam, set aside. Whisk together egg yolks and white wine over low heat until foaming; add butter, pouring in a steady stream and stirring constantly. Add lemon juice, Tabasco and salt and pepper. Stir and cook until thickened, about 5 minutes.

Seafood

Jambalaya

The Garrison House Inn

2 1/2 tablespoons good quality vegetable oil
2/3 cup cubed smoked ham
1/2 cup smoked pork sausage (Kielbasa)
1 cup chopped onion
2/3 cup chopped celery
1 large green pepper, in squares
3/4 cup cubed uncooked chicken
4 medium tomatoes, peeled and chopped
2 cloves garlic, minced
1/4 teaspoon Tabasco sauce or minced chili peppers to taste
2 bay leaves
3/4 teaspoon salt
3/4 teaspoon pepper
2 teaspoons dried oregano
2 teaspoons dried thyme
3/4 cup tomato sauce
2 1/2 cups chicken or seafood stock
1/2 cup chopped green onion
1 1/2 cup uncooked long grain rice
1/2 lb. shrimp, uncooked, shelled and deveined
3/4 lb. white fish, cubed (haddock, cod or halibut)

Preheat oven to 350°F. In a large, ovenproof saucepan add oil and sauté ham and sausage over medium heat for 3-5 minutes, stirring frequently. Add onion, celery and green pepper and sauté until softened. Add chicken, raise heat to high and cook 1 minute, stirring constantly. Add tomatoes and simmer 5 minutes, stirring often. Add garlic, Tabasco or red peppers, bay leaves, salt, pepper, oregano, thyme and tomato sauce and cook for 2 minutes, stirring.

Stir in stock and bring to a boil. Add green onion, rice and seafood. Stir gently and remove from heat. Cover and bake in preheated oven 20-30 minutes until all moisture is absorbed by rice. Remove bay leaves and serve. Serves 6.

Jumbo Shrimp Stuffed with Crab

Victoria's Historic Inn

1 1/2 cups chopped crab meat
3/4 cup cracker crumbs
1 small clove garlic, crushed
2 tablespoons melted butter
1/2 teaspoon chopped parsley
1/2 teaspoon seafood seasoning
20-24 jumbo shrimp, uncooked with shell (21-25 count)

Mix above ingredients except shrimp in a bowl with a fork and set aside. Cut shrimp lengthwise, flatten out and place a tablespoon of stuffing on top of each shrimp. Place on a baking sheet and cook in a preheated 400°F oven 4-5 minutes. Serve hot shrimp on a bed of rice. Serves 4-5.

Halibut with Tomato and Rosemary

The Halliburton House Inn

2-3 tomatoes
1 tablespoon fresh rosemary or 1/2 teaspoon dried
1 clove garlic minced
1 tablespoon olive oil
1 tablespoon lemon juice
salt and pepper to taste
4-6 halibut fillets

Combine tomatoes, rosemary, garlic, oil and lemon juice in a food processor and puree. Transfer to a saucepan and cook over medium heat until hot and slightly thickened. Keep Warm.

Broil halibut taking care not to overcook. To serve pour sauce over fish and garnish with fresh rosemary and lemon wedges. Serves 4-6

Sea Trout "Papillote"

Inn on the Lake

4-6 sea trout, 12 oz. each, cut in fillets
1/4 cup lemon juice
1 tablespoon Worcestershire sauce
salt and pepper to taste
1/2 cup butter
1/3 cup chopped fresh parsley
1 clove garlic, minced
2 teaspoons Worcestershire sauce
2 teaspoons lemon juice
4-6 sheets of parchment paper, 10 x 15 inches
2 green onions, chopped
1 cup sliced mushrooms
hollandaise sauce

Place fillets in shallow dish. Combine lemon juice, Worcestershire sauce, salt and pepper and brush this marinade over fillets. Set aside.

Combine butter, parsley, garlic and remaining Worcestershire sauce and lemon juice. Place one fillet, skin side down, on each piece of parchment paper. Divide butter mixture equally among the fillets and spread to edges of fish. Sprinkle green onions and mushrooms equally over fillets. Cover with remaining fillets, skin side up.

Wrap the fillets very tightly in the parchment paper and place on a cookie sheet. Bake at 375°F for 12-16 minutes, depending upon the thickness of fillets. Serve immediately in the parchment paper with hollandaise sauce on the side. Serves 4-6.

Use purchased parchment paper or brown paper that has been buttered or oiled and wrapped and folded tightly around food.

For hollandaise sauce recipe, see page 55.

Merluzzo in Bianco (Haddock in White Wine Sauce)

La Perla/San Remo

1 1/2 lb. haddock fillets
flour
olive oil
2 tablespoons butter
1 teaspoon minced garlic clove
1/2 cup sliced green onion
1/2 cup chopped onion
1/2 cup sliced red pepper
1/2 cup white wine
salt and pepper to taste
1/4 cup chopped fresh parsley
1/2 cup heavy cream (32% m.f.)
1/2 lemon

Remove any bones from fillets and cut into serving-sized portions. Dip fillets in flour to coat. Heat olive oil in skillet and quickly brown fish on both sides. Remove fish, set aside and remove oil from skillet. Add butter to skillet and sauté garlic and vegetables until tender. Add wine, salt, pepper and parsley. Bring to a boil, then add cream and bring back to a boil. Squeeze in juice from 1/2 lemon. Add cooked fish and simmer 5 minutes. Serve immediately. Yields 4-6 servings.

(The chef suggests using any leftover sauce to top steamed rice or toss it with noodles such as fettucine or linguine.)

Sole in Phyllo Pastry

Stanhope by the Sea

8 oz. package frozen phyllo pastry
2 eggs, beaten (egg wash)
1 1/4 lbs. small sole fillets
8-12 spinach leaves, washed, dried and trimmed
1 teaspoon chopped chives
salt and pepper to taste
3 tablespoons butter, melted

Thaw phyllo pastry in the refrigerator overnight. When working with the pastry remember that it dries quickly and should be covered with a clean, damp cloth.

Place a sheet of pastry on a dry surface. Brush with egg wash and place another sheet on top of the first. Repeat for a third sheet. With a sharp knife divide pastry sheets in half vertically and horizontally, making 4 equal rectangles. Cover with a damp cloth.

Divide the sole servings and spinach leaves between the 4 rectangles of pastry, alternating first spinach and then sole, until all sole and spinach are used. Season with chives, salt and pepper and brush with melted butter. Fold over pastry to form a triangle packet, moisten edges with egg wash, place on a buttered cookie sheet and brush packets with melted butter. Bake in a preheated 375°F oven until browned, approximately 10-12 minutes. Serves 4.

Fillet of Sole Amandine

The Algonquin

6 boneless fillets of sole, about 5 oz. each
1/2 cup flour
1/4 cup butter
juice of 2 lemons
1/3 cup sliced almonds

Dredge sole in flour, dusting off excess. Melt half the butter in a heavy skillet and brown the sole on both sides until golden. Place sole on a hot serving platter. Deglaze the pan with lemon juice, add the remaining butter and almonds, sauté until almonds are brown. Spoon lemon-almond mixture over fillets and serve. Yields 6 servings.

Broiled Mackerel with Mustard

La Poissonnière

3 whole mackerel, cleaned and filleted
2 tablespoons chopped fresh parsley
salt and pepper to taste
1/4 cup melted butter
2 teaspoons Dijon-style mustard
2 tablespoons lemon juice
lemon wedges for garnish

Prepare mackerel fillets. In a small bowl combine parsley, salt, pepper and half of the melted butter. Brush fillets with parsley butter.

Preheat broiler or barbeque and broil fish, 3-4 inches from heat source, for 5 minutes, turning once. Combine mustard, lemon juice and remaining melted butter and brush on fillets. Continue broiling fillets until cooked. Garnish with lemon wedges. Serves 4-6.

Fishcakes with Rhubarb Relish

Boscawen Inn

1 lb. dried salt cod
3 1/2 cups mashed potatoes
1/3 cup finely diced pork scraps (fat)
1 cup chopped onion
1 egg beaten
1/2 cup bread crumbs
rhubarb relish

Soak dried cod overnight in cold water. Change water, remove any bones and boil for 15 minutes, until soft. Drain fish and reserve.

In a skillet fry pork scraps and onion until pork is well browned and onions are softened. Combine all ingredients in a large bowl, blending gently. Shape mixture into approximately 8 individual cakes.

Panfry fishcakes in a buttered skillet until browned on both sides and heated through. Alternatively brush cakes with melted butter, sprinkle with paprika and broil in oven until browned on both sides and heated through. Serve with rhubarb relish. Serves 4-6.

Rhubarb Relish
8 cups finely chopped onions
4 cups boiling water
8 cups chopped rhubarb
3 cups cider vinegar
7 cups white sugar
2 teaspoons cinnamon
2 teaspoons ground cloves
2 teaspoons salt
1 teaspoon pepper

Scald onions in boiling water, drain and set aside. In a large saucepan bring onions, rhubarb, vinegar, sugar, cinnamon, cloves, salt and pepper to a boil. Reduce heat and simmer until thickened, about 3 hours, stirring frequently. Store in sterilized jars. Serve with fish or pork dishes. Yields 5-6 pints.

Poached Salmon Steaks with Dill Sauce

Victoria's Village Inn

4 cups water
1 cup dry vermouth
1 stalk celery with leaves, chopped finely
1 large carrot, sliced
1 medium onion, sliced
1 bay leaf
8 peppercorns
1/2 teaspoon salt
2 sprigs fresh parsley
4 salmon steaks, approximately 8 oz. each
dill sauce

Combine the water, vermouth, celery, carrot, onion, bay leaf, peppercorns, salt and parsley in a large saucepan and simmer 30 minutes. Place the salmon steaks in the liquid and gently simmer 12-15 minutes. Remove steaks with a slotted spatula to serving plates and serve with dill sauce. Yields 4 servings.

Dill Sauce
1/4 cup butter
1/4 cup flour
10 1/2 oz. can chicken broth
1/2 cup light cream (10% m.f.)
1 tablespoon dried dill weed or 2 tablespoons chopped fresh
2 teaspoons sugar
2 tablespoons white vinegar
1 egg yolk, beaten

Melt the butter in a saucepan and stir in the flour. Gradually mix in the chicken broth and cream. Continue to cook, stirring constantly until sauce thickens and bubbles. Add the dill, sugar and vinegar. In a separate bowl beat the egg yolk, stir a small amount of the hot mixture into the yolk, then beat the egg mixture into the sauce. When reheating, do not allow the sauce to boil. Serve over poached salmon steaks or with sliced roast lamb. Yields 2 cups.

Poached Atlantic Salmon

Shaw's Hotel

2-3 lbs. fresh salmon
cold water to cover fish
1 cup dry white wine
1/2 cup lemon juice
a few peppercorns
1 large carrot, diced
1 medium onion, sliced
1 stalk celery with top, sliced
1/4 cup chopped fresh tarragon
white wine sauce

Place salmon on a rack in a poaching pan. Cover with water, wine, lemon juice, peppercorns, carrot, onion, celery and tarragon. Bring to a boil, reduce heat and simmer, covered, 2 minutes per pound. Let stand in water one hour. Drain, peel and serve with warm white wine sauce. Serves 4-6.

White Wine Sauce
2 tablespoons butter
2 tablespoons flour
2/3 cup milk
1/3 cup heavy cream (32% m.f.)
2 tablespoons dry white wine
salt to taste
1 tablespoon chopped fresh parsley

Melt butter and stir in flour to form roux. Whisk in the milk, cream and wine. Cook over medium heat, stirring constantly until thickened. Adjust seasoning with salt and parsley. Serve warm over salmon. Yields 1 cup sauce.

Seafood Skibbereen

Zwicker's Inn

1 cup water
2/3 cup dry white wine
1/8 teaspoon dry mustard
1/8 teaspoon minced garlic
1/8 teaspoon salt
pinch of sugar
pinch of pepper
1 small piece bay leaf
1 large parsley sprig
1/3 cup shallots, sliced in thin rings
1/2 cup grated carrot (relatively long strips)
1/4 cup butter
1/4 cup flour
1 cup heavy cream (32% m.f.)
1 1/2 tablespoons plus 1/4 teaspoon Bailey's Irish Cream Liqueur
1 1/2 lbs. previously poached mixed seafood (lobster, shrimp, scallops etc.)

In a heavy-bottomed pot combine water, wine, mustard, garlic, salt, sugar, pepper, bay leaf, parsley and shallots. Boil gently 5 minutes. Add carrot and continue to cook an additional 5 minutes. Remove bay leaf and parsley. Strain mixture and reserve vegetables. Continue cooking the liquid until reduced to 1 1/4 cups and reserve.

In the same heavy-bottomed pot melt the butter, gently stir in the flour and cook slowly for 3 minutes. Whisk the cooking liquid, heavy cream and Bailey's Irish Cream into the flour mixture, bring to a boil to thicken, stirring constantly and being careful not to reduce. Add the reserved vegetables and seafood, heat through and serve in individual casserole dishes, on plates with steamed vegetables or rice or over homemade noodles. Serves 6.

Digby Scallops "Pines Fashion"

The Pines

2 tablespoons butter
2 boneless chicken breasts, cut in strips
6 large mushrooms, sliced
1 medium onion, finely chopped
1 clove garlic, finely chopped
1 lb. Digby scallops, sliced in half if large
4 tomatoes, peeled, seeded and chopped
2 oz. Cognac or brandy
1/3 cup lobster bisque
1/2 cup heavy cream (32% m.f.)
salt and pepper to taste

Melt butter in a large frying pan. Add chicken strips and stir fry gently 3 minutes. Add mushrooms, onion and garlic and cook 3 minutes, until vegetables are soft. Add scallops and chopped tomatoes and cook an additional 3 minutes. Warm Cognac or brandy slightly, pour over mixture and flambé. When flames die down, stir in the bisque and cream, simmering gently for 2-3 minutes. Season with salt and pepper and serve in individual scallop shells or over a bed of steamed rice. Yields 4 servings.

If lobster bisque is not available increase heavy cream to 2/3 cup.

Coquilles St. Jacques

Tara Manor Inn

1/4 cup butter, melted
2 small garlic cloves, minced
1/4 teaspoon white pepper
1/4 cup diced onion
1/4 cup diced green pepper
2 cups sliced fresh mushrooms
1 1/2 lbs. scallops
1/2 cup dry white wine
1 cup evaporated milk
2 teaspoons butter

1 tablespoon flour
1/4 cup grated Parmesan cheese

In melted butter, sauté garlic, pepper, onion, green pepper, mushrooms and scallops until scallops are opaque in appearance, 5-7 minutes. Transfer vegetables and scallops to a shallow serving dish and keep warm. Deglaze skillet with wine. Whisk in milk and simmer to reduce and thicken.

In the meantime blend together the butter and flour, forming two or three small balls. Add to sauce and continue to cook until thickened. Return scallop mixture to sauce, stirring to coat. Place in a shallow casserole or individual shells, sprinkle with grated Parmesan and broil until bubbly and browned. Serves 4-6.

Digby Scallops with Sauce Vièrge

Keltic Lodge

1 tablespoon butter
3 tomatoes, chopped
2 garlic cloves, minced
4 tablespoons olive oil
2 tablespoons wine vinegar
salt and pepper to taste
1 tablespoon each, fresh chervil, tarragon and parsley or 1 teaspoon dry
3 black olives, sliced
1 1/2 lbs. scallops
4 cups vegetable stock

In butter sauté tomatoes and garlic until softened. Add olive oil, vinegar, salt and pepper and heat but do not boil. Add herbs and olives and keep warm.

Steam scallops over vegetable stock for approximately 5 minutes. Do not overcook. Serve scallops topped with sauce. Serves 4-6.

(The chef serves this dish over cooked lentils.)

Seafood Casserole

Steamers Stop Inn

1 lb. haddock fillets
1/2 lb. scallops
1/2 lb. shrimp
1 tablespoon pickling spice
1 bay leaf
2 tablespoons lemon juice
1 cup water
1 cup chopped onion
1 cup chopped celery
1/4 cup butter
1/4 cup butter (second amount)
1/2 cup flour
2 1/2 cups milk
1/2 lb. Velveeta cheese, grated
dash each of curry powder and Tabasco sauce
salt and pepper to taste
1/2 lb. cooked lobster meat
1/4 lb. cooked crab meat
8-10 green pepper rings
1/4 cup Parmesan cheese

Cut haddock into bite-sized pieces, being careful to remove any bones. Rinse and clean scallops and shrimp, set aside. Tie pickling spices and bay leaf in a piece of cheesecloth to make a bouquet garni. Bring the lemon juice and water to a simmer in a large skillet, add the bouquet garni and assorted fish. Poach until just cooked, about 3 minutes. Remove seafood with a slotted spoon to a large bowl.

Sauté onions and celery in the first amount of butter until tender, 5-7 minutes. Scoop out the vegetables and set aside. Add the second amount of butter to the skillet and melt. Whisk in the flour, then stir in the milk and cheese. Cook sauce until thick and bubbly. Season with curry, Tabasco sauce, salt and pepper.

Carefully fold the cooked seafood chunks, onion and celery mixture into the sauce. Add the cooked lobster and crab. Arrange in a large, two-quart casserole or 8 individual dishes.

Bake in a 375°F oven until bubbly, about 20 minutes, depending upon the size of your serving dishes. Top with green pepper rings and sprinkle with Parmesan cheese. Return to oven and bake until browned on top. Serves 8.

Lobster Newburg

Marshlands Inn

lobster meat to serve 4
4 tablespoons butter
6-8 tablespoons medium sherry
1 1/2 cups heavy cream (32% m.f.)

Lightly sauté lobster in butter. Add sherry and cook on medium to medium-high heat for 1 minute. Remove lobster to an ovenproof casserole. Add cream to sherry and bring to a boil cooking until mixture is slightly thickened. Pour cream over lobster and bake in a 375°F oven for 10 minutes. Serve with vegetables or rice. Yields 4 servings.

Lobster Pie

Dundee Arms Inn

6 pastry rounds
5 tablespoons butter
1 leek, diced (white part only)
1 clove garlic, crushed
4 tablespoons flour
juice from lobster plus milk to make 2 cups
3-4 oz. ''Nippy'' old cheddar cheese, crumbled
salt and freshly ground pepper to taste
2 11-oz. cans frozen lobster meat

Prepare the pastry rounds in advance by rolling out pastry and cutting 6 rounds to cover the individual casseroles you plan to use. Prick and bake until golden brown in a 375°F oven, approximately 5 minutes. Cool and store, separated by pieces of waxed paper, until ready to use.

Melt butter in a large saucepan and sauté the leek and garlic until tender. With a slotted spoon, remove vegetables and set aside. Whisk the flour into the melted butter to form a roux. Drain the lobster meat and add enough milk to the lobster juice to measure 2 cups. Gradually stir the liquid into the roux and cook over medium heat, stirring constantly, until the sauce is bubbly and thick. Stir in the crumbled cheese and continue to cook until smooth. Add the leek-garlic mixture to the sauce and adjust seasonings.

Break the lobster into bite-sized pieces, being careful to remove any cartilage or shell. Fold into the cheese sauce. Place in 6 individual casseroles. To serve, bake in a 350°F oven for 20 minutes or until bubbly. Cover with baked pastry rounds and let stand a few minutes until the steam from the lobster warms the pastry. Yields 6 servings.

(This is a perennial favorite at the Dundee Arms Inn and the chef says it is easily prepared hours before serving time.)

Seafood Lasagne

The Compass Rose, N. B.

10 lasagne noodles
1 lb. spinach
4 eggs
1 lb. cottage cheese
salt and pepper to taste
1/8 teaspoon nutmeg
6 tablespoons butter
1 onion, chopped
1 clove garlic, crushed
1 tablespoon fresh dill
6 tablespoons flour
salt and pepper to taste
2 tablespoons sherry
3 cups light cream (10% m.f.)
1 cup grated Swiss cheese
1 1/2 lbs. seafood (lobster, scallops, tinned salmon or white fish in combination)
1/2 cup grated Parmesan cheese

Cook lasagne noodles until tender, drain and rinse under cold water. In boiling salted water, poach raw seafood until barely cooked. Drain and reserve. Briefly cook spinach, drain well and chop. Lightly beat eggs. In a large bowl combine eggs, spinach, cottage cheese, small amount of salt and pepper and nutmeg, mixing well.

Melt butter and sauté onion and garlic until limp. Add dill, flour, salt and pepper to taste and cook, stirring constantly, over medium heat for 1 minute. Whisk sherry and cream into flour mixture a little at a time until smooth and well blended. Cook, stirring constantly, until thickened. Add Swiss cheese and seafood and heat through.

Place half the noodles in a greased 9 x 13-inch lasagne pan. Spread half the spinach mixture over noodles and cover with half of the seafood mixture. Repeat. Top with Parmesan cheese and bake at 350°F for 45 minutes to an hour or until bubbly and well browned. Remove from oven and let stand 10-15 minutes before serving. Serves 8.

Gamberetti Alla Primavera

The Lunenburg Inn

6 tablespoons butter
1 medium onion, chopped
2 small garlic cloves, chopped
1/2 cup tarragon wine
3/4 teaspoon caraway seeds
2 tablespoons cornstarch
2 tablespoons warm water
1/3 cup milk
1 cup heavy cream (32% m.f.)
salt and pepper to taste
2 cups assorted vegetable pieces (red and green pepper strips, broccoli, cauliflower, carrot medallions, peas, mushrooms, etc.)
4 servings fettucine
4 cups fresh shrimp, shelled and deveined
fresh parsley to garnish, if desired

Melt butter in a saucepan and sauté onion and garlic until limp and opaque but not brown. Add wine and caraway and simmer 1 minute. Mix together the cornstarch and water, add to the saucepan and thicken 1 minute, stirring constantly. Slowly add the milk and cream to the pan and bring back to almost a boil. Season with salt and pepper.

In the meantime, steam or microwave the vegetables until crisp tender. Cook the fettucine until al dente (cooked but firm) and drain. Steam or microwave shrimp until cooked.

Divide pasta between 4 serving plates. Top with vegetables, shrimp and sauce. Garnish with chopped parsley, if desired. Yields 4 servings.

Tarragon Wine
Add 1 teaspoon dried tarragon to dry white wine and let stand in a covered jar for 24 hours.

Seafood Pasta

The Inn at Bay Fortune

1/2 lb. fresh mussels
1/2 lb. fresh clams
3/4 lb. cod or sole fillets in bite-sized pieces
1/2 lb. scallops
2 tablespoons finely diced shallots
6 tablespoons butter, clarified
2/3 cup dry white wine
2/3 cup fish velouté sauce
2/3 cup heavy cream (32% m.f.)
1/2 teaspoon dried tarragon
1/4 teaspoon dried basil
salt and pepper to taste
pasta to serve 4 (fettucine or linguine)
freshly grated Parmesan cheese
chopped fresh parsley for garnish
lemon wedges

Steam and shuck the mussels and clams and set aside. Sauté fillets, scallops and shallots in clarified butter in a large saucepan. Set seafood aside and deglaze pan with wine. Add the velouté sauce, cream, tarragon and basil. Bring to a boil to thicken slightly, stirring constantly. Add seafood and season with salt and pepper.

Cook pasta and divide between 4 serving plates. Spoon seafood sauce over pasta, sprinkle with grated Parmesan and garnish with chopped parsley and lemon wedges. Yields 4 servings.

Fish Velouté Sauce
2 tablespoons butter
2 tablespoons flour
1 cup fish stock

Melt butter in the top of a double boiler over simmering water. Add flour, blending well. Whisk in stock and cook until thickened, stirring constantly. Yields 1 cup sauce.

Fettucine Alla Marinara

The Lunenburg Inn

1/4 cup olive oil
2 cloves garlic, minced
3/4 cup dry red wine
28 oz. can tomatoes, chopped
28 oz. can tomato sauce
1 cup thinly sliced celery
2 teaspoons dried oregano
2 teaspoons dried thyme
2 teaspoons fennel seeds
2 teaspoons dried parsley
1/4 teaspoon cayenne pepper (optional)
6 lbs. fresh mussels
1 cup water
1 teaspoon salt
fettucine to serve 6-8
freshly grated Parmesan cheese (optional)

In a large, heavy-bottomed saucepan, heat olive oil and sauté garlic until golden. Add wine, tomatoes, tomato sauce, celery, oregano, thyme, fennel, parsley and cayenne and bring to a boil, stirring occasionally. Lower heat and simmer until celery is cooked, approximately 25-30 minutes.

Scrub and pick over mussels, discarding any that are cracked or do not close when tapped. Bring water and salt to a boil, add mussels and steam 5-6 minutes until mussels open. Shell mussels, rinse in warm water and drain well. Add to tomato sauce.

In the meantime, cook enough fettucine to serve 6-8. Serve sauce over fettucine noodles and top with grated Parmesan cheese, if desired. Serves 6-8.

Vegetables

Beets Dijonnaise

Halliburton House

1/2 cup heavy cream (32% m.f.)
1 heaping teaspoon Dijon-style mustard
2 cups cooked beets

Mix cream and mustard until well blended in a medium-sized saucepan. Add beets, sliced or halved, and simmer until cream is reduced and sauce has thickened and clings to the beets, approximately 8 minutes. Serve immediately. Serves 4.

The chef says this "is guaranteed to make beet lovers out of the most jaded palate."

Beets with Pineapple

The Amherst Shore Country Inn

14 oz. can pineapple chunks, packed in their own juice
1 tablespoon cornstarch
1 tablespoon brown sugar
1 tablespoon butter
1 teaspoon lemon juice
2-3 cups cooked beets, whole, halved or diced

Drain the pineapple chunks, reserving juice, and set aside. Stir together the pineapple juice, cornstarch, sugar, butter and lemon juice over medium heat until slightly thickened. Add cooked beets and a few pineapple chunks and bring to serving temperature. Serves 4-6.

Broccoli with Lemon Bechamel Sauce

The Amherst Shore Country Inn

1 large head broccoli, trimmed
2 1/2 tablespoons butter
2 1/2 tablespoons flour
1/2 cup chicken stock
1/2 cup heavy cream (32% m.f.)
1/2 tablespoon grated lemon zest
salt and pepper to taste
1/4 cup sour cream

Trim and wash broccoli, cook until crisp tender, drain and transfer to a serving dish. In the meantime melt the butter in a heavy saucepan, whisk in the flour, stock, cream and zest. Cook over medium heat, stirring constantly until thickened. Adjust seasoning with salt and pepper. Remove from heat and stir in sour cream. Pour over broccoli. Serves 4-6.

Broccoli in Cream and Herbs

The Amherst Shore Country Inn

1 bunch broccoli spears
1/4 cup heavy cream (32% m.f.)
1 tablespoon butter
salt and pepper to taste
1/2 teaspoon dry or 1 teaspoon chopped fresh tarragon, sweet basil or marjoram

Cook broccoli spears until tender, drain well and return to saucepan. Add cream, butter, salt, pepper and herbs to saucepan and bring back to a boil. Stir gently to coat broccoli and slightly reduce the cream mixture. Serves 4-6. (This works well with cauliflower or other vegetable medley.)

Potato Almond Croquettes

Inverary Inn

4 medium potatoes
salt and pepper to taste
pinch of ground nutmeg
2 tablespoons butter
1 1/2 teaspoons finely chopped fresh parsley
milk or cream to moisten dry potatoes (optional)
1 cup milk
1 egg
flour for dredging
slivered almonds
vegetable oil for frying

Boil potatoes as for mashed potatoes. Drain well and mash. Season with salt, pepper, nutmeg, butter, parsley and milk or cream if extra moisture is required. Cover and refrigerate until well chilled. When completely cooled, shape mixture into small balls or ovals and refrigerate.

Make egg wash with milk and beaten egg. Assemble croquettes by dredging in flour, shaking off excess, dipping and coating in egg wash and rolling in slivered almonds. Deep fry croquettes, a few at a time, in vegetable oil heated to 360°F, until golden brown. Drain on paper towels, keep warm in low oven until served. Serves 4.

Baked Stuffed Potatoes

Victoria's Village Inn

4 large baking potatoes
3/4 cup sour cream
2 tablespoons butter
1 medium egg, beaten
1/4 teaspoon salt
freshly ground pepper
2 tablespoons chopped chives
2-3 tablespoons brandy
fresh parsley for garnish

Scrub and pierce potatoes and bake at 425°F until tender, from 40 to 60 minutes depending upon the size. Slit tops and scoop out potato, being careful to keep the shell intact. Mash the potato in a bowl, mix in the sour cream, butter, beaten egg, salt, pepper, chives and brandy. Carefully place the mixture back into the potato shells and reheat in a 400°F oven for 10 minutes. Serve garnished with a sprig of parsley, if desired. Serves 4.

Egyptian Rice

Stanhope by the Sea

2 1/2 tablespoons butter
1 very small garlic clove, minced
1 cup brown rice
1 1/4 cups boiling water
3 tablespoons onion soup mix
1 cup boiling water
1 1/2 tablespoons white wine
1 teaspoon butter
1/4 cup dried currants (preferably red)
2 tablespoons slivered almonds

In a cast iron or Corning Ware casserole, melt butter and sauté garlic. Add rice and slowly cook until butter is absorbed, about 3-4 minutes. Add 1 1/4 cups boiling water. When moisture is absorbed (7-8 minutes), gently stir in onion soup mix under the lowest heat possible. Add 1 cup boiling water, stir, cover casserole and place in a preheated 375°F oven until moisture is gone, about 40-45 minutes. Check during last 15 minutes and add more water, if necessary. Stir in wine.

Heat butter in a small saucepan and sauté currants and almonds over low heat until currants are plump and almonds are golden. Fold currants and almonds into rice mixture. Serves 6.

Nova Scotia Maple Syrup Baked Beans

Liscombe Lodge

1 lb. dry white beans (2 1/2 cups)
6 cups water
6 slices bacon, cut in 2-inch pieces
1 small onion, chopped
1/2 teaspoon dry mustard
1 1/2 teaspoons salt
1/2 cup dark maple syrup
2 tablespoons brown sugar
2 tablespoons butter

Bring the beans and water to a boil in a large saucepan and boil for 2 minutes. Remove from heat and let stand, covered, for an hour. Return to a boil, reduce heat and simmer, covered, for 40 minutes. Drain, reserving cooking liquid.

Place half of the bacon in the bean crock and add beans. In a separate bowl combine the reserved cooking liquid, onion, dry mustard, salt and maple syrup. Pour over the beans and top with remaining bacon. Bake, covered at 325°F for 3 hours. From time to time check beans and add a small amount of water if they appear dry.

Cream together the brown sugar and butter. Sprinkle over the beans and bake an additional hour, uncovered. Serves 6-8 as a main course.

Brandied Carrots

The Amherst Shore Country Inn

fresh carrots to serve 6
2 tablespoons butter
2 tablespoons brandy
2 teaspoons sugar
chopped fresh parsley or chives for colour contrast, if desired

Cut carrots into preferred shape and cook until crisp tender. Melt butter, add brandy and sugar. Pour over hot carrots, stir to coat evenly and sprinkle with parsley or chives for garnish. Serves 6.

Pickled Carrots

Amherst Shore Country Inn

3 large carrots
1/2 cup egg-based mayonnaise
1 teaspoon dried parsley or 1 tablespoon chopped fresh
1 tablespoon finely chopped onion
1/2 teaspoon prepared horseradish
1 tablespoon water
buttered bread crumbs

Peel carrots and cut on the diagonal in rounds or into medium-sized sticks. Blanch carrots until partially cooked and drain well. Place carrots in a casserole dish. Mix mayonnaise, parsley, onion, horseradish and water together and stir into carrots. Cover casserole and bake in a preheated 350°F oven for 20 minutes. Remove cover after 10 minutes and sprinkle carrots with bread crumbs. Serves 6.

Sweet and Sour Sauerkraut

The Compass Rose, N. S.

1 quart sauerkraut
1/4 lb. bacon
4 teaspoons Worcestershire sauce
8 tablespoons brown sugar
salt and pepper to taste
1 large apple, pared and chopped
1/4 cup dry white wine

Drain sauerkraut in a colander. Cook bacon until crisp in a Corning Ware casserole or heavy-bottomed saucepan. Drain off fat. Place half the sauerkraut over the bacon, sprinkle with half the Worcestershire and half the brown sugar. Repeat the layers of sauerkraut, sugar and sauce. Season with a scant amount of salt, if desired, and pepper. Spread chopped apple over sauerkraut and sprinkle with wine. Bring to a boil, reduce heat to low and steam, covered, for 15 minutes until crisp tender. Serves 4.

Turnips with Brown Sugar and Sherry

Amherst Shore Country Inn

1 medium turnip
salt and pepper to taste
1 tablespoon butter
1 tablespoon brown sugar
1 tablespoon dry sherry

Peel turnip and slice into broad strips. In a large saucepan bring water to a rolling boil, add turnip and blanch two minutes. Drain. Place turnip in a shallow casserole, season with salt and pepper and dot with butter. Cover tightly with foil and bake in a preheated 350°F oven for 20-25 minutes. Mix together the brown sugar and sherry, pour over turnip and stir to coat. Continue baking, covered, an additional 10 minutes or until turnip is tender. Serves 4-6.

Zucchini Provençale

The Captain's House

2 tablespoons olive oil
2 small onions, chopped
2 cloves garlic, crushed
16 oz. can whole tomatoes, drained
1/3 cup dry white wine
1 tablespoon tomato paste
1/2 teaspoon thyme
salt and pepper to taste
2 medium zucchini, halved lengthwise, seeded and cut in thin slices

In a small saucepan heat the oil and sauté the onion and garlic until tender; stir in the drained tomatoes, breaking them with a fork. Add the wine, tomato paste and thyme and simmer until slightly thickened. Season with salt and pepper and stir in zucchini slices. Simmer until zucchini is crisp tender. Serves 4-6.

Pies and Cakes

Acadian Apple Pie

The Algonquin

1/2 cup raisins
3/4 cup apple juice
2/3 cup water
1/2 cup sugar
4 medium-large apples, peeled and sliced
1/4 teaspoon salt
1 teaspoon lemon zest
1/2 teaspoon lemon juice
1 tablespoon butter
1/4 teaspoon cinnamon
2 tablespoons cornstarch
3/4 cup walnut pieces
9-inch pie plate lined with sweet dough
1/4 cup melted butter
1/2 cup sugar
1/2 cup (scant) flour
1/2 cup (scant) rolled oats
whipped cream or maple syrup for topping, if desired

Rinse and dry raisins. In a saucepan, combine raisins, apple juice, 1/3 cup water, sugar, apples, salt, lemon zest and juice, 1 tablespoon butter and cinnamon. Bring to a boil and gently cook over medium heat. Stir in cornstarch which has been dissolved in 1/3 cup water and boil for three minutes. Remove from heat and stir in walnuts. Spoon mixture into prepared pie shell.

Mix together melted butter, 1/2 cup sugar, flour and oats and sprinkle over pie. Bake in a preheated 350°F oven for 35-45 minutes until cooked and browned. Serve with whipped cream or maple syrup. Serves 6.

Sweet Dough
2/3 cup sugar
3/4 cup soft butter
1 egg
2 cups flour

With a mixer, whip sugar and butter until light and fluffy. Add egg and continue to beat. Mix in flour, roll into 2 balls.

Roll out dough and fit into shallow pie plate. This recipe will make 2 single-crust pie shells. May be halved using a small egg or 1/2 of a large egg which has been whisked with a fork in a cup.

Angel Peach Pie

The Normaway Inn

1 1/2 cups graham cracker crumbs
1/3 cup melted butter
5 egg whites
1/4 teaspoon salt
1/2 teaspoon cream of tartar
peaches, fresh or canned, sliced and drained
1 1/2 cups heavy cream (32% m.f.)
2 tablespoons sugar
1 cup coconut, toasted

Combine graham crumbs and butter and press into a 9-inch pie plate. Make meringue by beating egg whites, salt and cream of tartar until stiff peaks form. Pour into crust, spreading evenly to the sides and bake in a preheated 275°F oven for 1 1/4 hours. Cool.

Arrange sliced peaches on top of cooled meringue. Whip cream and sugar and spread over peaches, top with toasted coconut. Serves 6-8.

Maple Inn Apple Pie

The Maple Inn

pastry to line a 10-inch glass pie plate
8 cups peeled, diced apples
1/4 cup butter
1/4 cup sugar
2 tablespoons cornstarch
1/4 cup maple syrup
3/4 cup brown sugar
1/2 cup flour
1/2 teaspoon freshly grated nutmeg
1/4 cup butter, cut in chunks
whipped cream to top, if desired

Line a pie plate with pastry and crimp edges. Sauté apples in butter for two minutes. Sprinkle apples with mixture of sugar and cornstarch and continue to cook, stirring gently to ensure apples are well coated. Pour maple syrup over apples and stir. Apples should be tender, not soft.

Spoon apples into pie shell, Prepare topping by combining brown sugar, flour, nutmeg and butter with a pastry blender. Sprinkle evenly over the apples. Bake in a preheated 400°F oven for 25 minutes, reduce oven temperature to 350°F and continue cooking for 20 minutes. Cool and serve with a spoonful of whipped cream that has been flavoured with maple syrup, if desired. Serves 6-8.

This original recipe by innkeeper Kathy Boles earned her a second place in the Taste of Nova Scotia Contest that selected pies to participate in *Yankee* magazine's Great New England Pie Contest in Boston in the fall of 1989.

Pastry
2 cups flour
1/2 teaspoon salt
1 cup shortening
5-6 tablespoons ice water

Combine flour and salt in a mixing bowl. Cut shortening into the flour with a pastry blender or 2 knives until mixture is the size of large peas. Do not over mix. Sprinkle cold water over flour mixture and blend with a fork until absorbed. Form into a ball and roll out on a floured surface. Makes a 10-inch open pie or a 9-inch lattice pie.

Coconut Cream Pie

Steamers Stop Inn

1/2 cup sugar
1/3 cup cornstarch
1/4 teaspoon salt
3 cups milk
2 egg yolks, lightly beaten
3 tablespoons butter
1 teaspoon vanilla
1 cup coconut (sweetened angel flake)
pastry for 9-inch pie shell
1/2 cup heavy cream (32% m.f.)
1 teaspoon sugar

In a saucepan, combine sugar, cornstarch and salt, then gradually stir in milk. Cook and stir over medium heat until mixture boils and thickens. Cook an additional 2 minutes. Remove from heat.

Stir a small amount of hot mixture into egg yolks, return yolks to hot mixture and cook 2 minutes, stirring constantly. Remove from heat, add butter, vanilla and coconut. Cool to room temperature and pour into a cooked 9-inch pie shell. Cover with waxed paper or plastic wrap so that a crust will not form on pie top and refrigerate.

At serving time, garnish with sweetened whipped cream and a few flakes of toasted coconut, if desired. To toast coconut, place on a cookie sheet in a 350°F oven until lightly browned, about 5 minutes. Serves 6-8.

Sour Cream Rhubarb Pie

Compass Rose, N.B.

pastry to line a 10-inch pie plate
4 cups cubed rhubarb
1 1/2 cups sugar
1/3 cup flour
1 cup sour cream
1/2 cup flour
1/2 cup brown sugar
1/4 cup butter, softened

Prepare pastry and line a 10-inch pie plate. Arrange rhubarb in unbaked pie shell. Combine sugar and 1/3 cup flour, stir in sour cream and pour mixture over the rhubarb. Combine 1/2 cup flour, brown sugar and butter until crumbly. Sprinkle over pie. Bake in 450°F oven for 15 minutes, reduce heat to 350°F and cook for an additional 30-40 minutes until fruit is tender, filling is set and topping is golden. Serves 6-8.

Rhubarb Pie Deluxe

The Bright House

pastry to line a 9-inch pie plate
2 tablespoons dry bread crumbs
1 teaspoon brown sugar
4 cups diced rhubarb
1/2 cup sugar or less for a tart pie
1/8 teaspoon salt
1 teaspoon grated lemon rind
2 teaspoons lemon juice
2 eggs, lightly beaten
3/4 cup sugar
1 teaspoon cornstarch

Prepare pastry and line a 9-inch pie plate. Sprinkle crumbs and brown sugar over pastry.

Combine rhubarb, 1/2 cup sugar, salt, lemon rind and juice and spread in pie shell.

Blend eggs, 3/4 cup sugar and cornstarch and pour over rhubarb. Preheat oven to 425°F and bake for 15 minutes, reduce heat to 325°F and bake until custard is set and rhubarb is soft, approximately 35-45 minutes. Serves 6.

Glazed Strawberry Pie

Steamers Stop Inn

pastry for 9-inch pie plate
1 quart fresh strawberries
1 cup sugar
3 tablespoons cornstarch
1/4 teaspoon salt
1 teaspoon lemon juice
1 1/2 tablespoons butter
whipping cream to garnish

Prepare the pie shell, bake and cool. Clean and hull the berries and cut in half. Cover pastry with a layer of berries, distributing evenly.

Combine sugar, cornstarch and salt in a saucepan. Crush the remaining berries (should be about 2 cups) and slowly blend into sugar mixture. Cook over medium heat until thickened and smooth. Reduce heat and cover saucepan, continue to cook for 5 minutes. Remove from heat and stir in lemon juice and butter. Pour over berries in pie shell being careful to cover them completely. Refrigerate at least 4 hours until set and serve covered with whipped cream, if desired. Serves 6.

Ohio Lemon Pie

Mountain Gap Inn

3 large lemons
2 cups sugar
1 teaspoon salt
4 eggs
pastry for 9-inch, 2-crust pie
vanilla ice cream or whipped cream, if desired

Carefully grate the 3 lemons, reserving the zest. Peel the lemons of all remaining pith. Thinly slice lemons, remove seeds and place slices in a large bowl. Stir in the sugar, salt and grated zest and let stand, refrigerated, between 2 and 24 hours.

Beat eggs and stir into the lemon mixture. Prepare pastry and line a 9-inch pie plate. Pour the lemon mixture into the pie shell, being careful to distribute the fruit evenly. Roll out left-over pastry and cut into strips 1/2 - 3/4 inches wide. Alternate strips over the pie at 1-inch intervals to form a woven lattice top. Press edges of pastry strips to lower crust and trim. Bake at 425°F for 10 minutes, then lower temperature to 325°F and bake an additional 45 minutes. Serve chilled, topped with vanilla ice cream or whipped cream, if desired. Serves 6-8.

Pastry chef Pamela MacIntosh says this tart lemon pie originated in a Mennonite community near Kitchener-Waterloo, Ontario.

Banana Layer Cake

The Quaco Inn

2/3 cup butter
1 1/4 cups brown sugar
2 eggs
1 teaspoon vanilla
1 1/4 cups mashed banana (3 medium)
2 cups flour
2 teaspoons baking powder
1 teaspoon baking soda
1/2 teaspoon salt
1/2 cup sour milk
cream cheese icing

Cream butter and sugar until light and fluffy. Add eggs, one at a time, beating well after each addition. Add vanilla and mashed banana.

Sift together flour, baking powder, soda and salt. Add flour mixture and sour milk to batter alternately in 2 additions. Pour batter into 2 8-inch round cake pans which have been greased and floured. Bake in a preheated 350°F oven for 30-35 minutes until a toothpick inserted in centre of cake comes out clean. Cool 10 minutes and remove from pans. Frost with cream cheese icing.

Cream Cheese Icing
4 oz. cream cheese, softened
1/4 cup butter, softened
3 cups icing sugar, sifted
1/2 teaspoon vanilla
1/4 teaspoon lemon juice

Cream together cheese and butter until well blended. Gradually beat in icing sugar, vanilla and lemon juice until desired consistency is reached. Yields enough for an 8-inch layer cake.

Old-fashioned Apple Cake

The Telegraph House

1 cup creamed honey
3/4 cup butter
2 eggs
1 teaspoon vanilla
2 1/4 cups white flour
2 teaspoons cinnamon
1 teaspoon baking soda
1 teaspoon baking powder
pinch of salt
2 cups thinly sliced, peeled apples
1/2 cup chopped nuts (optional)
whipped cream, if desired

Beat together honey and butter until creamy, about 3 minutes. While still beating, add eggs, one at a time, and vanilla.

Sift together flour, cinnamon, soda, baking powder and salt. Stir flour mixture into honey and butter and combine well. Gently stir in apple and chopped nuts. Turn mixture into a greased and floured 9-inch square pan, keeping batter higher at the sides. Bake in a preheated 350°F oven until cake pulls away from the sides of the pan, about 40-50 minutes. Serve with whipped cream, if desired.

Butter Tarts

The West Point Lighthouse

1 cup brown sugar
1/3 cup butter, melted
1 teaspoon vanilla
1 egg
2 tablespoons milk
10 unbaked pastry tarts

Mix together brown sugar, butter and vanilla. Stir in the egg and milk. Pour into prepared small tart shells and bake at 400°F for 15 minutes.

Blueberry Coffee Cake

Gowrie House

1/2 cup plus 1 tablespoon butter, softened
1 2/3 cups sugar
3 eggs
3 1/2 cups flour
1 teaspoon salt
1 teaspoon soda
1 1/4 cups rich milk (1 cup whole milk plus 1/4 cup light or heavy cream)
2 teaspoons lemon extract
3-4 cups fresh blueberries
1 tablespoon sugar
1 1/2 teaspoons cinnamon
3 tablespoons melted butter
juice of a lemon

Cream butter and sugar until light and fluffy. Add eggs and beat well.

In a separate bowl combine flour, salt and soda. Combine rich milk and lemon extract. Add flour mixture and rich milk alternately to batter in 3 additions, beating well. Gently fold blueberries (if using frozen berries, thaw and drain well) into batter. Pour into a greased and floured 9 x 13-inch pan.

Mix together sugar and cinnamon and sprinkle over the top of the cake. Bake at 350°F for 50-60 minutes until centre springs back when touched lightly. Remove cake from oven.

Combine melted butter and lemon juice and brush over top of cake.

Carrot Cake with Warm Cheese Sauce

The Galley

1 cup vegetable oil
2 cups white sugar
4 eggs
2 cups flour
2 teaspoons baking powder
1/2 teaspoon soda
1 1/2 teaspoons cinnamon
1/2 teaspoon nutmeg
1 teaspoon salt
3 cups grated carrot
1/2 cup raisins
1/2 cup chopped walnuts
1 cup chopped, drained pineapple
warm cream cheese sauce

Beat together the oil and sugar until frothy. Add eggs, one at a time, mixing after each addition until smooth.

In a separate bowl sift together flour, baking powder, soda, cinnamon, nutmeg and salt. Add the dry ingredients to the egg mixture, a little at a time, mixing until batter is smooth. Fold in the carrots, raisins, walnuts and pineapple. Pour into a greased 9 x 13-inch pan and bake at 350°F for 60-65 minutes. Cool on a wire rack and serve with warm cream cheese sauce.

Warm Cream Cheese Sauce
4 oz. cream cheese at room temperature
3 tablespoons butter at room temperature
1 1/2 - 2 cups icing sugar
1/2 teaspoon vanilla
1 tablespoon lemon juice

Cream together the cheese and butter in a medium-sized mixing bowl. Slowly sift in the icing sugar and continue beating until smooth and fully incorporated. Stir in vanilla and lemon juice. At serving time warm sauce for 1 - 1 1/2 minutes on high in a microwave oven and spoon over individual servings of cake.

Breads and Muffins

Cape Smokey Blueberry Pancakes

Keltic Lodge

2 eggs
1/4 cup vegetable oil
1/4 cup honey
2/3 cup yogurt
1/2 cup milk
1/2 cup apple cider
1 2/3 cups enriched white flour
1/2 teaspoon salt
1 1/2 teaspoons baking soda
1/2 teaspoon cinnamon
blueberries

Beat eggs. Add oil, honey, yogurt, milk and apple cider and beat well. Mix together flour, salt, baking soda and cinnamon. Add flour mixture to yogurt mixture, stirring only until combined.

Preheat a greased skillet to 400°F. Dollop batter on skillet, sprinkle blueberries on pancakes and when bubbles form on uncooked side of pancakes, flip and continue cooking until done. Serve with butter and maple syrup. Serves 4-6.

Brown Bread

The Marshlands Inn

1/2 cup lukewarm water
1 1/2 tablespoons yeast
1/2 cup rolled oats
1/2 cup graham flour
4 tablespoons shortening
1 1/2 teaspoons salt
1/4 cup brown sugar
1/4 cup molasses
1 cup boiling water
3/4 cup cool water
5 1/2 - 6 cups enriched white flour

Combine 1/2 cup lukewarm water and yeast in a bowl, stir and let stand 10 minutes until bubbly.

In a large bowl combine oats, graham flour, shortening, salt, sugar and molasses. Pour 1 cup boiling water over oat mixture and beat, melting shortening. Beat in cool water and when this mixture is lukewarm, beat in the yeast. Gradually add the enriched flour, incorporating enough to make a slightly sticky dough. Knead 6-8 minutes on a lightly floured board until smooth and elastic. Shape into a ball and place in a lightly greased bowl, turning once to grease surface. Cover and let rise in a warm place until double, about 1 hour.

Punch down dough, divide in half and let rest 10 minutes. Shape into 2 loaves and place in greased 9 x 5 x 3-inch loaf pans. Cover and let rise until double, about 45-60 minutes.

Bake in a preheated 375°F oven for 40 minutes or until done. Check last 15 minutes and cover loosely with foil if browning too much. Remove from pans and cool on wire racks. Brush tops with melted butter. Yields 2 loaves.

Fentunta

The Inn at Bay Fortune

1 package of dry yeast
1/2 cup warm water (110°F)
1/4 cup olive oil
2 cups hot water
6 cups all purpose flour
2 teaspoons salt
1 tablespoon oregano
1/2 teaspoon thyme
1 teaspoon crumbled rosemary

Combine yeast and warm water in a small bowl. Set aside until yeast is activated, about 10 minutes.

In a large bowl combine olive oil and hot water. Beat in 3 cups flour and then beat in the yeast mixture. Stir the salt, oregano, thyme and rosemary into the remaining flour and then mix it into the dough, a little at a time, until dough is moderately stiff. Turn out onto a floured surface and knead until smooth and satiny, 8-10 minutes. Shape into a ball and place in a lightly greased bowl, turning once to grease surface. Cover and let rise in a warm place until double, about 1 1/2 hours.

Punch down and shape into 2 double loaves. Place in 2 greased 4 x 8-inch loaf pans. Cover and let rise until double, about 1 hour.

Bake in a preheated 450°F oven 20-25 minutes until bread is browned and sounds hollow when tapped. Serve warm. Yields 2 double loaves.

White Bread

Marshlands Inn

1/2 cup warm water
1 teaspoon sugar
1 tablespoon yeast (generous)
1 1/3 cups hot water
1/3 cup shortening
1 tablespoon salt
3 tablespoons sugar
1 1/3 cups cold water
8 cups flour

Combine warm water and 1 teaspoon of sugar in a small bowl. Sprinkle yeast over water, stir and let stand 10 minutes until bubbly.

In a large bowl pour hot water over shortening, salt and sugar. Stir until shortening melts. Add cold water and when mixture is lukewarm, add the yeast and beat. With a wooden spoon beat in enough flour to form a batter. Gradually add remaining flour to form a sticky dough. Turn out dough on a lightly floured surface and knead until smooth and elastic, about 8-10 minutes. Shape into a ball and place in a lightly greased bowl, turning once to grease surface. Cover and let rise in a warm place until double, about 1 hour.

Punch down dough, turn out and divide into 4 equal portions. Shape into 4 rounded loaves and place in two 9 x 5 x 3-inch greased loaf pans. Cover and let rise until double, about 45-60 minutes.

Bake in a preheated 400°F oven for 30 minutes, turning loaves after 15 minutes. Remove from pans and cool. Makes 2 double loaves. These may also be baked as rolls in 400°F oven for 20 minutes, turning rolls after 10 minutes.

"Lobster" Rolls

Compass Rose, N.B.

1 tablespoon dry yeast
1 teaspoon sugar
1/2 cup lukewarm water
1/3 cup sugar
1 teaspoon salt
1/3 cup oil
1 2/3 cups warm water
5-6 cups white flour

Dissolve yeast and 1 teaspoon sugar in lukewarm water and let rise to at least 1 cup in volume. Combine sugar, salt, oil and warm water in a large bowl and whisk briskly. Add yeast mixture to other liquids and beat. Gradually add flour, 1 cup at a time, beating after each addition, until you need to combine the remainder with your hands.

Knead dough until smooth and slightly sticky, about 5 minutes. Place dough in a greased bowl and turn to cover ball with oil. Cover and let rise for 45 minutes in a warm, draft-free place.

Punch down and shape into rolls of your choice in greased pans. Cover and let rise again for 45 minutes.

Bake in a preheated 375°F oven for 12-15 minutes until lightly golden. Brush tops with butter, remove from pans and cool on wire racks. Yields 2 dozen cloverleaf-style rolls.

At the Compass Rose on Grand Manan Island, the rolls are formed into an oblong shape and used for their famous lobster rolls.

Morning Glory Muffins

Mountain Gap Inn

2 cups flour
1 cup sugar
2 teaspoons baking powder
2 teaspoons cinnamon
1/2 teaspoon salt
1/2 cup raisins
1/2 cup chopped nuts
1/2 cup coconut
3 eggs
1 cup vegetable oil
2 teaspoons vanilla
2 cups grated carrot
1 apple, peeled and finely chopped

Combine first 8 dry ingredients in a large bowl. In another bowl beat eggs, oil and vanilla. Blend carrots and apple into egg mixture. Add liquid mixture to dry ingredients and stir only until combined. Fill greased or paper-lined muffin tins 2/3 full. Bake at 400°F for 18-20 minutes, until golden on top. Remove from tins and cool. Makes 2 dozen muffins.

Carrot Pineapple Muffins

The Innlet Café

1 1/4 cups white flour
1/2 cup whole wheat flour
1 teaspoon baking powder
3/4 teaspoon salt
1 teaspoon cinnamon
1 teaspoon baking soda
1 pinch ground nutmeg
1 cup grated carrot
2 eggs
2/3 cup vegetable oil
1/2 cup crushed pineapple, well-drained
1 teaspoon vanilla
1/2 cup liquid honey

In a large bowl combine flours, baking powder, salt, cinnamon, soda and nutmeg and blend well. Stir in grated carrot.

In another bowl beat eggs. Add oil, pineapple, vanilla and honey to eggs and beat. Add egg mixture to flour mixture stirring only until combined. Grease or line large muffin tins and fill cups to level. Makes 7 very large or as many as a dozen regular-sized muffins. Bake in a preheated 350°F oven for 20-25 minutes (depending upon size of muffins), until a knife inserted in the centre comes out clean.

Tea Biscuits

Liscombe Lodge

3 cups white flour or 1 1/2 cups white and 1 1/2 cups graham flour
2 tablespoons baking powder
3/4 teaspoon salt
2 teaspoons sugar
1/2 cup shortening
1 1/2 cups milk

Sift together flour, baking powder, salt and sugar. Blend in shortening with a pastry blender until fine. Add milk and stir with a fork until it forms a soft dough.

Turn dough onto a lightly floured surface and knead gently 8-10 times. Pat to desired thickness and cut with a floured cookie cutter or glass. Bake on an ungreased cookie sheet at 425°F for 12-15 minutes.

Johnny Cake

The Quaco Inn

1 cup flour
1/4 cup sugar
1 teaspoon baking powder
3/4 teaspoon salt
1/2 teaspoon soda
1 cup cornmeal
1 tablespoon melted butter
2 tablespoons molasses
1 egg, beaten
1 cup buttermilk or sour milk

In a large bowl combine the flour, sugar, baking powder, salt, soda and cornmeal. In a small bowl beat together the butter, molasses, egg and milk. Stir liquid mixture into the dry ingredients, blending well. Bake in a greased 8-inch square pan at 400°F for 20-25 minutes. Serve warm.

Scottish Oatcakes

Telegraph House

1/2 cup boiling water
1/2 teaspoon soda
1 1/4 cups sugar
2 cups rolled oats
2 cups flour
2 cups bran flakes
1 teaspoon baking powder
1 teaspoon salt
1 1/4 cups shortening

Add soda to boiling water and let stand until cool. In a large bowl mix together sugar, oats, flour, bran flakes, baking powder and salt. Cut in shortening with pastry blender or fingers. Add soda and water to mixture and blend.

Refrigerate batter 10 minutes. Roll out on a floured surface to 1/4-inch thickness. Cut in squares and place 1/2-inch apart on greased cookie sheet. Bake at 450°F, for 8-10 minutes, until golden brown.

Blomidon Inn Bread

Blomidon Inn

2/3 cup warm (110°F) water
2 teaspoons sugar
2 1/2 tablespoons dry yeast
1 cup quick-cooking rolled oats
1/2 cup cornmeal
1 cup molasses
1 teaspoon salt
1 tablespoon shortening
2 cups very hot water
6 cups all purpose flour

Place warm water, sugar and yeast in a bowl. Stir to mix and let stand 10 minutes.

In the meantime combine rolled oats, cornmeal, molasses, salt, shortening and hot water in a large bowl and cool to lukewarm.

Combine yeast and oats mixture. Beat in flour, 2 cups at a time, until dough is firm, not sticky. Turn out on a floured surface and knead, adding additional flour if necessary, until dough is smooth and elastic, about 5 minutes.

Grease 2 bread pans. With greased hands, form dough into 4 small loaves or 2 large loaves, making sure dough is greased all over. Place in prepared pans. Cover and let rise in a warm, draft-free place until double, about 1 1/2 - 2 hours.

Bake in a preheated 350°F oven until browned. Loaves should sound hollow when tapped. Turn out on wire racks to cool. Yields 2 loaves.

Desserts

Fresh Fruit Shortbread

The Pines

1 2/3 cups flour, sifted
1/2 cup unsalted butter, in cubes at room temperature
1 cup icing sugar, sifted
pinch of salt
2 egg yolks, beaten
1 teaspoon vanilla or lemon essence
1 quart strawberries or raspberries
1/4 cup sugar, if desired

Place flour in a medium bowl, add butter pieces and work into flour with fingers or a pastry blender. Sift icing sugar into butter mixture and blend. Add salt, egg yolks and flavouring of choice, mixing well. Divide dough into two parts and roll out to 1/8-inch thickness on a lightly floured surface. Cut into 2-inch rounds and bake on an ungreased cookie sheet in a 350°F oven 10-12 minutes or until slightly golden. Carefully remove with a spatula to a wire rack and cool.

Prepare berries of choice, halving the large ones. Remove a few berries to a bowl, crush to make a sauce and add sugar, if desired. Roll remaining berries in the sauce.

To assemble, place four shortbread rounds on four dessert plates, top each with a few berries, add another shortbread round, more berries and then a third round. As a finishing touch, top the final shortbread with a berry or two and pour a ribbon of the sauce around the top. Yields 4 servings.

Amaretto Cheesecake

Boscawen Inn

1 1/3 cups Graham cracker crumbs
1/3 cup melted butter
1/4 cup crushed almonds
1/4 cup brown sugar
2 cups cream cheese, softened
1/2 cup sour cream
2/3 cup sugar
2 large eggs
1 teaspoon almond extract
1 teaspoon Amaretto liqueur
1 cup sour cream
2 tablespoons sugar
2 tablespoons Amaretto liqueur
5 tablespoons flaked almonds, toasted

Combine Graham cracker crumbs, butter, crushed almonds and brown sugar in a bowl. Mix well and press into the bottom and slightly up the sides of a 9-inch springform pan. Bake in a preheated 350°F oven for 5 minutes.

Meanwhile, with a mixer, cream the softened cream cheese. Blend in the 1/2 cup sour cream and 2/3 cup sugar. Beat in the eggs, one at a time. Add almond extract and 1 teaspoon Amaretto and beat until smooth. Pour cream cheese mixture into the baked crust, return to 350°F oven and bake 30-35 minutes. Remove cheesecake from oven and let sit for 5 minutes.

Increase oven temperature to 450°F. In a mixing bowl, combine 1 cup sour cream, 2 tablespoons sugar and 2 tablespoons Amaretto and blend well. Pour sour cream mixture over cheesecake, spreading evenly to edges. Sprinkle with toasted almonds. Return to oven and bake a further 10 minutes. Remove cake from oven, let stand until it reaches room temperature and then refrigerate at least 3-4 hours before serving. Serves 10-12.

Lemon Cheesecake

Shaw's Hotel

1 1/3 cups crushed chocolate wafers
1/3 cup butter, melted
1/4 cup sugar
16 oz. cream cheese, softened
3 medium eggs
1/2 cup sour cream
2/3 cup sugar
2 tablespoons lemon juice
1 cup sour cream
4 tablespoons brown sugar
2 tablespoons lemon juice
fruit in season or whipped cream, if desired

Mix together wafer crumbs, melted butter and 1/4 cup sugar and press into the bottom of a greased 9-inch springform pan. Set aside.

Cream the cheese until fluffy. Add eggs, one at a time, beating until smooth. Mix in 1/2 cup sour cream, 2/3 cup sugar and lemon juice. Pour into the prepared springform pan and bake in a 350°F oven for 35 minutes.

Combine 1 cup sour cream, brown sugar and lemon juice, spread evenly over the cheesecake and return to the oven for an additional 10 minutes. Turn off heat and leave cheesecake in the oven until it is firm and the oven is cool. Chill and top with seasonal fruit or whipped cream, if desired. Yields 10-12 servings.

Crème de Menthe Cheesecake

The Manor Inn

2 cups crushed chocolate wafers
1/2 cup butter, melted
1 lb. cream cheese, softened
1 cup sugar
1/3 cup Crème de Menthe liqueur
3 eggs
3 cups sour cream
4 squares semi-sweet chocolate
1/2 cup sour cream

Combine chocolate wafer crumbs and melted butter and press into bottom and sides of a 10-inch springform pan.

Beat together cream cheese, sugar and Crème de Menthe just until smooth. Add eggs and beat on low speed just until blended. Fold 3 cups sour cream into mixture and turn into prepared crust. Bake in a preheated 375°F oven for 60-70 minutes until skewer inserted in centre comes out clean. Cool on wire rack.

While cake is cooling, melt chocolate in the top half of a double boiler over hot water. Cool chocolate for 5 minutes. Whisk 1/2 cup sour cream into chocolate and pour over top of cheesecake, spreading to edges. Chill 4-5 hours before serving. Serves 12.

Plain Cheesecake with Variations

The Compass Rose, N.S.

1/3 cup butter, melted
1/4 cup sugar
1/4 teaspoon vanilla
2/3 cup flour
24 oz. cream cheese, softened
1 cup sugar
5 eggs
1 1/2 teaspoons vanilla

To make crust, cream butter and 1/4 cup sugar until light and fluffy, add vanilla and mix in flour to form a dough. Press dough into the bottom of a greased 9-inch springform pan.

Beat the cream cheese until soft, add 1 cup sugar and cream well. Add eggs and vanilla and continue to beat until smooth. Pour over dough in pan and bake on the centre rack of a 350°F oven for 50-55 minutes. Cool on a wire rack.

Cheesecake Sundae
3/4 cup sugar
1/3 cup cocoa
3 tablespoons cornstarch
1/2 cup water
1/4 cup light corn syrup
1/4 cup butter
1 teaspoon vanilla
chocolate ice cream (superior quality)
whipped cream
cherries and crushed nuts for garnish

Make chocolate sauce by combining sugar, cocoa and cornstarch in a small saucepan. Blend in water and corn syrup. Cook over medium heat, stirring constantly, until mixture boils. Continue to stir and cook an additional minute. Remove from heat and stir in butter and vanilla.

Top a slice of plain cheesecake with a scoop of chocolate ice cream. Drizzle chocolate sauce over the ice cream and cheesecake. Place a spoonful of whipped cream on the back of the cheesecake and another on top of the ice cream, add a cherry and crushed nuts.

Cheesecake with Glazed Fresh Fruit Topping
assorted fresh fruit (strawberries, raspberries, kiwi, etc.)
1/4 cup red currant or apple jelly
1 tablespoon water

Decorate the top of cool, plain cheesecake with assorted fresh fruit. Melt red currant or apple jelly, thinning slightly with a tablespoon of water, and brush over fruit. Chill.

Fudge Mint Torte

Milford House

12 oz. semi-sweet chocolate pieces
1 cup butter
1 1/2 cups brown sugar
4 eggs
1 1/2 cups sifted flour
2 cups heavy cream (32% m.f.)
1/3 cup Crème de Menthe liqueur (green)
1/4 cup confectioners' sugar (icing sugar)
chocolate curls for garnish, if desired

Prepare three 9-inch round layer cake pans by greasing pans, lining with waxed paper and greasing the paper.

Combine the chocolate pieces and butter in a saucepan and melt over low heat. Transfer to a large bowl and beat in the sugar, then add the eggs, one at a time, beating after each addition. Mix in the flour until well blended. Divide batter evenly between the three pans and bake at 350°F for 20-25 minutes. Cool in pans on a wire rack for 10 minutes, then invert and peel off the waxed paper and cool cakes completely.

Prepare the filling by whipping the cream until stiff. Beat in the liqueur and sugar. To assemble stack and fill layers using 1/3 of the filling between each layer and remainder over top. Garnish with chocolate curls, if desired. Yields 8-10 servings.

Lemon Hazelnut Flan

Silver Spoon

1/2 cup sugar
2 cups flour
2/3 cup unsalted butter (cold)
1 egg
1/2 cup sugar
1/4 cup unsalted butter
juice and grated rind of 2 large lemons
5 eggs
1 cup natural hazelnuts, coarsely ground
whipped cream as garnish

Combine 1/2 cup sugar and flour, mixing well. Add 2/3 cup cold unsalted butter, piece by piece, combining with fingers until well blended and granular. Add egg and blend well to bring pastry together. Pat dough into a 10-inch fluted flan pan, distributing evenly over bottom and sides. Bake at 375°F for 14-15 minutes until lightly golden. Cool.

In the top of a double boiler over hot water, combine 1/2 cup sugar, 1/4 cup butter, lemon juice and rind. Stir until sugar is dissolved and mixture is hot. Remove top of double boiler from stove and quickly beat eggs into hot mixture, one at a time. Return sauce to stove over hot water and, whisking constantly, cook until thick. Cool.

Fold hazelnuts into lemon sauce and pour into baked flan shell, spreading evenly. Bake at 375°F for 15-20 minutes, until slightly puffed. When cool, unmold from flan pan and either decorate around border with rosettes of whipped cream or serve individual slices with a dollop of whipped cream on the side. Serves 8-10.

Hazelnut Meringue Torte

Gowrie House

whites of 4 large eggs
1/4 teaspoon salt
1/4 teaspoon cream of tartar
1 cup granulated sugar
1 cup hazelnuts, coarsely ground
4 cups heavy cream (32% m.f.)
3 squares semi-sweet chocolate
2 tablespoons icing sugar
2 tablespoons ground coffee (finest grind)

In a large bowl whip the egg whites with salt until foamy, add cream of tartar and continue whipping until stiff. Gradually add granulated sugar, a tablespoon at a time, and continue beating until meringue is very stiff and glossy. Carefully fold in hazelnuts, reserving 2 tablespoons for garnish. Draw two 7-inch circles on a foil-covered cookie sheet and either pipe or spread the meringue on these circles. Place in a preheated 275°F oven and bake for 1 hour. Turn off heat and leave for at least 1 additional hour until dry.

To make chocolate filling, stir and melt 1/4 cup of the heavy cream and the chocolate in a small, heavy-bottomed saucepan over low heat. Remove from heat and cool slightly. Carefully spread this mixture on the smooth sides of cooled meringue layers and place in the refrigerator for 15 minutes to set.

To make coffee cream frosting, whip remaining cream. Add 2 tablespoons icing sugar and 2 tablespoons finely ground coffee. Do not use instant coffee. Use this filling between layers and on sides and top of torte. Sprinkle with reserved hazelnuts. Refrigerate at least 4 hours before serving. Yields 8-10 servings.

Marvelous Mocha Cake

Heron Country Inn

1 1/4 cups chocolate wafer cookie crumbs (about 24 cookies)
1/4 cup sugar
1/4 cup butter, melted
8 oz. package cream cheese
14 oz. can Eagle Brand sweetened condensed milk
2/3 cup chocolate syrup
2 tablespoons instant coffee, dissolved in 1 teaspoon hot water
1 cup heavy cream (32% m.f.), whipped

In a small bowl combine the cookie crumbs, sugar and melted butter. Press firmly into the bottom and up the sides of a 9-inch springform pan. Chill.

In a large mixing bowl beat the cream cheese until fluffy, add the sweetened condensed milk and chocolate syrup, blending well. Dissolve coffee granules in hot water in a small cup, add to cream cheese mixture and mix well. In a separate bowl whip the cream, then fold into the cream cheese mixture. Pour into prepared crumb pan, cover and freeze 8 hours or until firm. Garnish with additional crumbs, if desired.

At serving time, unmold on a plate and cut in wedges. Return any leftover cake to the freezer. Serves 8-10.

Rossmount Cookie Crumb Pie

Rossmount Inn

3 cups heavy cream (32% m.f.)
1 tablespoon sugar
1 package chocolate chip cookies (600 g)
1/2 cup coffee liqueur
chocolate curls
strawberries or maraschino cherries, well drained

Whip cream and sugar until very stiff. In a 10-inch springform pan place a layer of cookies. Sprinkle with a third of the liqueur. Top cookie layer with a layer of cream, spreading evenly with a spatula. Continue layering cookies, liqueur and cream until pan is nearly full, ending with a layer of cream. Using a pastry bag with a star tip, decorate top by piping on remaining cream. Cover with plastic wrap and refrigerate overnight.

At serving time, garnish with chocolate curls and fruit. Yields 10-12 servings.

Brownies

The West Point Lighthouse

2 eggs
1 cup sugar
1/2 cup butter, softened
1 teaspoon vanilla
1 cup flour
1 teaspoon baking powder
1/4 teaspoon salt
1/2 cup cocoa
boiling water
1/2 cup walnuts, chopped

Beat eggs and sugar one minute. Add butter and vanilla to egg mixture and beat until light and fluffy. Sift together flour, baking powder and salt. Add enough boiling water to cocoa to make 1 cup.

Alternately add dry and liquid ingredients to egg mixture in two additions. Stir in nuts. Bake in a greased 8 inch square pan at 350°F for 30 minutes. Cool in pan before icing.

Chocolate Butter Icing
2 tablespoons butter, softened
1/2 teaspoon vanilla
few grains of salt
2 tablespoons cocoa
1-1/2 cups icing sugar
2 tablespoons cream or milk

Cream together butter, vanilla and salt. Combine cocoa and icing sugar and beat into butter mixture, alternately with cream.

Chocolate Truffle Cake

Inverary Inn

chocolate cake, baked in a 9-inch springform pan
Grand Marnier liqueur to brush cake, if desired
8 squares semi-sweet chocolate
1/2 cup heavy cream (32% m.f.)
2 1/2 tablespoons Grand Marnier
3 cups heavy cream (32% m.f.), whipped
icing sugar for dusting
crème Anglaise sauce

Line a 9-inch springform pan with waxed paper. Divide the baked and cooled cake in half and place the first layer in the prepared pan. Brush with Grand Marnier, if desired.

Melt chocolate, stir in 1/2 cup cream and liqueur and cool. Prepare whipped cream and fold into cold chocolate mixture. Spread half the chocolate cream mixture over the cake being careful to make layers flat and smooth. Place the second layer of cake on top of the cream and refrigerate until set. Remove cake from springform pan and decorate top and sides with remaining chocolate cream mixture.

At serving time, dust cake with icing sugar and serve each slice with a thin layer of crème Anglaise sauce.
Yields 10-12 servings.

Crème Anglaise Sauce
1/2 cup heavy cream (32% m.f.)
1/2 cup milk
yolks of 2 large eggs
4 tablespoons icing sugar
almond, vanilla or orange flavouring

Heat the cream and milk in the top of a double boiler over hot water but do not boil. Whisk together the yolks and icing sugar. Stir a small amount of the hot mixture into the yolks, return yolks to hot mixture and cook gently until mixture lightly coats the back of a spoon. Remove from heat and flavour to taste. Cover with plastic wrap and chill. Yields 1 cup sauce.

Zabaglione

La Perla/San Remo Restaurant

5 egg yolks
5 tablespoons sugar
1/3 cup Marsala wine
1/3 cup white wine
lady fingers or fresh fruit

Put egg yolks and sugar in top of a double boiler and whisk briskly until well combined. Add wines and whisk to blend.

Place top of double boiler over boiling water and whisk constantly until thick and foamy, about 4-5 minutes. Serve immediately in champagne glasses with lady fingers or fresh fruit. Serves 4.

Coupe Royale Glace

Captain's House

2 cups seasonal fruit (melon chunks, green grapes, oranges, etc.)
1/4 cup Grand Marnier liqueur
1 litre French vanilla ice cream
1/2 cup heavy cream (32% m.f.), whipped with 1 tablespoon sugar

Toss fruit with liqueur and reserve. Divide ice cream among 4 parfait glasses, top with fruit and a dollop of whipped cream. Serves 4.

Hot Fudge Dessert

Telegraph House

1/3 cup melted shortening
1 egg
3/4 cup sugar
1 cup flour
4 tablespoons cocoa
1 teaspoon baking powder
1/4 teaspoon salt
1 cup milk
1 cup brown sugar
3 tablespoons cocoa
2 1/2 cups boiling water
whipped cream for garnish

Melt shortening and cool slightly. In a mixer beat egg and sugar, add cooled shortening and beat again. Stir together flour, cocoa, baking powder and salt and add to egg mixture alternately with the milk.

Grease an ovenproof 2-quart casserole and pour in batter. Combine brown sugar and cocoa and whisk in boiling water. Pour sauce over batter. Bake in a preheated 375°F oven for 45-55 minutes until done. Serve warm or cold topped with whipped cream. Serves 6.

Apple Crisp

The Bright House

6 apples, peeled and sliced
1/2 cup apple juice
1/2 teaspoon ground cinnamon
1 tablespoon butter
3/4 cup flour
3/4 cup brown sugar
3/4 cup rolled oats
3/4 cup grated medium Cheddar cheese
1/2 cup butter

Grease a 1 1/2 quart baking dish and fill with sliced apples. Pour apple juice over apples, sprinkle with cinnamon and dot with 1 tablespoon butter.

Combine flour, brown sugar, oats, cheese and 1/2 cup butter until crumbly. Sprinkle flour mixture over apples. Bake in a preheated 350°F oven for 30-40 minutes until top is browned and apples are soft. Serves 6-8.

Bananas Foster

Victoria's Historic Inn

2 tablespoons butter
4 tablespoons brown sugar
2-3 bananas, cut in quarters
pinch of cinnamon
1 tablespoon banana liqueur
3 tablespoons rum or brandy
vanilla ice cream

Combine butter and brown sugar in a saucepan. Cook over medium heat until almost caramelized, 3-5 minutes. Add quartered bananas and cook until barely tender. Add cinnamon and liqueur. Stir gently.

To flambé, warm rum or brandy, pour over the bananas (do not stir) and carefully light. Spoon bananas and sauce over vanilla ice cream balls and serve immediately. Serves 4-6.

Mud Pie

Harbourview Inn

1-2/3 cups crushed chocolate wafers
1/2 cup melted butter
1 litre coffee ice cream
3 tablespoons butter
1/3 cup cocoa
1/3 cup heavy cream (32% m.f.)
2/3 cup sugar
1 teaspoon vanilla
1 cup heavy cream (32% m.f.)
2 tablespoons sugar
1 teaspoon vanilla
chocolate curls

Mix together chocolate wafers and melted butter and press into the bottom and sides of a pie plate. Bake crust 375°F for 8 to 10 minutes. Cool completely. Slightly soften ice cream and spread into pie shell. Freeze until firm, 1 to 2 hours.

In saucepan, over medium heat, melt 3 tablespoons butter. Gradually whisk cocoa, 1/3 cup cream and 2/3 cup sugar into butter, and continue stirring until mixture boils. Remove from heat, stir in 1 teaspoon vanilla and cool completely. Spread chocolate over ice cream pie and return to freezer. Whip 1 cup cream with 2 tablespoons sugar and 1 teaspoon vanilla until stiff. Remove pie from freezer, garnish with whipped cream and chocolate curls. Serves 6-8.

Inns and Restaurants of New Brunswick

The Algonquin

If you think the days of "the grand old hotels" are past, think again. Sited high atop a hill overlooking the historic town of St. Andrews lies the Algonquin, a massive turreted hotel featuring 200 guest rooms, two golf courses, tennis, swimming, cycling and superb cuisine.

The resort town of St. Andrews was founded by United Empire Loyalists in 1783, many of the first residents having dismantled their homes in Maine to reassemble them across Passamaquoddy Bay in British New Brunswick. Today more than half of the town's buildings are over 100 years old and a walking tour of the tree-lined streets is a pleasant way to spend a morning. Other attractions of St. Andrews include the Huntsman Marine Science Aquarium-Museum, with its "please touch tank," West Point blockhouse, the historic Charlotte County Courthouse, boat tours of the bay and whale watching cruises. From nearby St. George, a toll auto ferry operates seasonally to Deer Island and another toll ferry transports you to Campobello Island, site of the Roosevelt International Park and summer home of the late President Franklin Delano Roosevelt.

Savour the fresh sea air, relax and enjoy the delicious cuisine of the Algonquin through its season May to October.

The Algonquin
St. Andrews by the Sea
New Brunswick
EOG 2XO
(506) 529-8823

Benoit's

Benoit's, in the heart of downtown Fredericton, N.B., is a small, intimate restaurant specializing in traditional French cuisine. The restaurant is decorated in a blue, black and peach art-deco style with crisp white linens and off-Broadway graphics.

Owners John Charles Belzile, Benoit Tremblay and chef Yvon Durand pay special attention to using fresh local ingredients in season. The menu is extensive and includes seafood, meat, poultry, pork, lamb and game entrées.

Benoit's is open year round, Monday to Friday (noon to 2 p.m. and 5 to 11 p.m.), Saturday and Sunday (5 to 11 p.m.). Reservations are recommended and all major cards are accepted.

Benoit's
536 Queen Street
Fredericton, N. B.
E3B 1B9
(506) 459-3666

The Compass Rose

The Compass Rose consists of two charming houses, furnished in antique pine and located close to the ferry wharf at North Head, Grand Manan Island, N. B. This remote island, the largest of New Brunswick's Fundy isles, is a two-and-a-half hour ferry trip from Black's Harbour and is a haven for bird watchers, artists, hikers and photographers.

The inn offers overnight accommodations in nine rooms and serves breakfast, lunch, afternoon tea and dinner in a dining room which opens to a long deck overlooking the sea. Everything is prepared on premises: Wednesday night is "lobster night" and a gourmet dinner is served at a single sitting Saturday evenings. The inn is open seasonally, May to October. Reservations are recommended and Visa is accepted.

The Compass Rose
Innkeepers: Cecilia Bowden & Linda L'Aventure
North Head
Grand Manan Island, N. B.
EOG 2MO
(506) 662-8570
Off season - (506) 357-3726 or (416) 921-7157

Heron Country Inn

The Heron Country Inn is a beautiful three-storey home, built in 1913 as a church manse. It is located at New Mills, N. B. on the shores of the beautiful Bay of Chaleur.

Ten guest rooms, colour co-ordinated in pastels, are furnished with antique or period pieces. Quilts, plants and lace curtains make the inn a quiet respite and the public dining room highlights homemade dishes such as chicken pot pie, seafood casserole and salmon steaks. All the ingredients are fresh and procured locally.

The bilingual staff at the Heron Country Inn can help you plan a complete vacation. Beautiful Charlo Falls and boat cruises to Heron Island with its miles of secluded beaches ideal for birdwatching, windsurfing and canoeing are but a few of the local attractions.

The Heron Country Inn is open seasonally and accepts Visa or Master Card.

Heron Country Inn
Site 13 Box 10
New Mills, N. B.
EOB 1MO
(506) 237-5306

La Poissonnière Restaurant

Located at Grande-Anse, N.B. in a north eastern area of the province known as the Acadian Peninsula, La Poissonnière Restaurant offers local residents and travellers the very best in local seafood.

Husband and wife team Rhonda Jen and Richard Chiaisson prepare a menu of fish available on the local market as well as a wide assortment of dishes to please the "land lubber's" palate. The most popular menu item, however, is "the catch of the day" when Chiaisson, who is an instructor at the Culinary Institute of Canada in Charlottetown, P. E. I. during the academic year, prepares such species as shark, lump fish, angelfish, shad or sturgeon.

The restaurant is open seasonally, mid June to mid September, serving breakfast, lunch and dinner daily. Visa, American Express and Master Card are accepted.

La Poissonnière Restaurant
484 rue Acadie
Route ll
Grande-Anse, N. B.
EOB 1RO
(506) 732-2000

The Marshlands Inn

The Marshlands Inn in Sackville, N. B. has been a landmark in the restaurant and accommodations business since 1935. Currently operated by John and Mary Blakely, Marshlands comprises two stately manors and a recently renovated coach house with a total of 25 rooms. All rooms are elegantly decorated with antiques and offer either private or shared baths.

Marshlands is known for its peaceful intimacy, with gardens and lawns, quiet parlours, dormer windows and stately dining room.

The inn takes its name from the Tantramar marshes that surround the town of Sackville. This area is along one of the main North American flyways for bird migration and huge sightings of geese and ducks are often observed as they come to rest on the marshes each spring and fall.

Marshlands Inn operates year round and all major credit cards are accepted.

Marshlands Inn
P. O. Box 1440
Sackville, N. B.
EOA 3CO
(506) 536-0170

The Quaco Inn

THE QUACO INN

When fire swept the Fundy village of St. Martins at the turn of the century, many of the stately old homes were lost. Fortunately the residence of the Skillen family, merchants during those prosperous days of sail and shipbuilding, survived. Today, innkeepers Eric and Marilyn Jackson have restored the home to its former grandeur.

Open year round, the Quaco Inn provides nine guest rooms, each named after former shipbuilding families of the area. In fact, each room is decorated with photographs and furniture from the homes of its namesake.

Hearty breakfasts are served to overnight guests and dinner is offered to guests and the public by advance reservation only. Each evening a choice of two entrées is offered in a homestyle reminiscent of a visit to grandmother's house for Sunday dinner.

St. Martins is New Brunswick's "well kept secret." Less than an hour's drive from Saint John, the village borders a three-and-a-half mile beach featuring unique rock formations, caves and stretches of sand. A visit to the Quaco Inn is ideal for sunbathing, birdwatching, sketching and relaxing.

The Quaco Inn
St. Martins, N. B.
EOG 2ZO
(506) 833-4772

The Rossmount Inn

The Rossmount Inn

At the Rossmount Inn you step back in time to the romantic Victorian era. The inn, a three-storey manor house with 16 guest rooms, is part of a private 87-acre estate at the foot of Chamcook Mountain, overlooking the Passamaquoddy Bay. The estate provides scenic hiking, nature trails, a large pool and spectacular panoramic views.

The inn's dining room provides superb homecooked food and good wines in a smoke-free atmosphere. The Victorian decor is complemented by the high ceiling and fine old fireplace, but the focal point is an alcove of three stained glass windows taken from an 18th century English chapel.

At Rossmount, the rooms are distinctive and spacious, furnished with unique antiques from all over the world, and the dining room features fresh fish and seafood, plus several meat entrées each day. Visa and Master Card are accepted.

The Rossmount Inn
Innkeepers: Robert & Lynda Estes
St. Andrews by the Sea, N. B.
EOG 2XO
(506) 529-3351

Shadow Lawn Country Inn

Shadow Lawn Country Inn

The Shadow Lawn Country Inn was built in 1871 by James E. Robertson, a prosperous Saint John merchant. Nestled near the Kennebecasis River at Rothesay, N. B., this multi-roomed Victorian structure was used as a summer home until the late 1940s.

Innkeepers Pat and Marg Gallagher offer overnight accommodations in eight elegantly appointed guest rooms. The mahogany-panelled lounge, sitting rooms and dining rooms are large and inviting. Dinner and breakfast are served to guests as well as the general public by advance reservation only. In addition, the lawns, gardens and patio make the Shadow Lawn an ideal place for receptions and special occasion events.

The inn is open year round and credit cards are not accepted.

The Shadow Lawn Country Inn
P. O. Box 41
Rothesay, N. B.
EOG 2WO
(506) 847-7539

Steamers Stop Inn

Steamers Stop Inn at Gagetown, N. B., is a charming and warm country inn, offering excellent cuisine in several formal dining rooms and accommodations in seven guest rooms.

Located on scenic route 102, 65 miles north of Saint John and 40 miles south of the capital city Fredericton, Gagetown boasts many attractions, including weavers, potters and several craft emporiums. History buffs can visit the Queens County Museum, which occupies the house where Father of Confederation Samuel Leonard Tilley was born in 1818, or stroll among the moss-covered tombstones of Loyalists in St. John's Anglican churchyard.

The inn is open year round and, because of its location on the banks of the Saint John River, is accessible to both the boating and motoring public. The inn can accommodate group parties and is an excellent "getaway" for small business meetings.

Steamers Stop Inn
Innkeeper: Pat Stewart
P. O. Box 155
Gagetown, N. B.
(506) 488-2903

Tara Manor Inn

TARA MANOR INN

Tara Manor, once the home of father of Confederation Sir Charles Tupper, is an elegant estate situated on 20 acres overlooking the town of St. Andrews by the Sea, N. B.

Elegant gourmet dining in the "Evening Star" dining room awaits guests and the public from 6 to 9 p.m. daily. Specialities include New Brunswick cream of fiddlehead soup, fresh seafood and an array of meat entrées. The broad lawns, woodlands and hedgegrows which provide sanctuary and shelter for an infinite variety of bird life are a delight for visitors, while the blue waters of the ocean sparkle close by.

Tara Manor is open from the end of May through mid October. Visa, Master Card and American Express cards are accepted.

Tara Manor Inn
Innkeepers: Norman & Sharon Ryall
St. Andrews by the Sea, N. B.
EOG 2XO
(506) 529-3304

Inns and Restaurants of Nova Scotia

Amherst Shore Country Inn

Tucked away in the northeastern corner of mainland Nova Scotia, this small inn offers five guest rooms, two cottages and gourmet dining with a view of the twinkling lights of all three Maritime provinces – Nova Scotia, New Brunswick and, in the distance, Prince Edward Island.

Everything is prepared on premises and innkeeper Donna Laceby does all her own cooking and baking. Donna has mastered the technique of using just the proper amounts of herbs, spices or liqueurs to enhance but never overwhelm her dishes.

Dinner is served nightly, by advance reservation only, at a 7:30 p.m. sitting. The menu changes each day with a choice of meat or seafood entrée and either a rich or light dessert. Choices may include crab bisque, stuffed sole, Cornish game hens with a cranberry and wild rice stuffing, blueberry flan or mincemeat trifle. The first person to make dinner reservations helps Donna decide what to prepare for that evening!

The Amherst Shore Country Inn is open May through Thanksgiving. Visa and Master Card are accepted.

Amherst Shore Country Inn
Innkeepers: James & Donna Laceby
R R # 2 Amherst
Lorneville, N. S.
B4H 3X9
(902) 667-4800

The Blomidon Inn

Situated in the university town of Wolfville in Nova Scotia's Annapolis Valley, the Victorian-styled Blomidon Inn was built in 1877 by Captain Rufus Burgess, a descendant of the New England Planters. Burgess made his fortune as a ship owner, sailing his fleet from nearby Kingsport. He directed his captains to bring exotic timber as ballast on their return voyages – these woods were used to create the magnificent entrance hall and stairway of the inn. Plaster cornices, dados and marble fireplaces were fashioned by Italian craftspeople.

The mansion was a private residence until the 1940s when it first opened its doors as a hostelry. In the 50s and 60s it was a home for Acadia University students but in 1980 was restored to its original elegance.

There are two dining rooms at Blomidon Inn. The larger main dining room is furnished in fine mahogany Chippendale chairs with a fireplace for cool evenings and a bay window for warm. The smaller library dining room is a favorite spot for intimate dinners or small groups. The menu is limited yet changes daily and great care is given to the century-old recipes such as chicken Elizabeth, cream of cauliflower soup or apple dumplings with nutmeg sauce.

The inn is open daily, with Visa and Master Card accepted, and reservations are suggested.

Blomidon Inn
Innkeepers: James & Donna Laceby
127 Main Street
Wolfville, N. S.
BOP 1XO
(902) 542-2291

Boscawen Inn

Boscawen Inn is a restored Victorian mansion situated in the historic fishing town of Lunenburg, N. S. The home, a dowry gift to Edna Rudolph from her father in 1888, sits high on a hill overlooking the front harbour.

This elegant inn features 18 bedrooms ranging in size from small cozy alcoves to large rooms with four-poster beds and sitting areas that overlook the port.

Lunenburg town and environs offer the traveller a host of ocean and land-based activities.

The restaurant at Boscawen Inn is open seven days a week for breakfast, lunch and dinner. The season runs from May to October 30. Visa and Master Card are accepted.

Boscawen Inn
Innkeepers: Ann & Michael O'Dowd
150 Cumberland Street
Lunenburg, N. S.
BOJ 2CO
(902) 634-3325

The Bright House

Situated close to historic Sherbrooke Village on Nova Scotia's eastern shore, the Bright House was built in 1850. This large frame building with its yellow clapboard siding opened to the public as a restaurant in 1975.

Hosts Wynneth and Gordon Turnbull offer their guests country meals with a difference. Many traditional English dishes, such as roast of beef with Yorkshire pudding and steak and kidney pie, are found on the menu. In addition, dinner begins with marvelous homemade wholewheat bread and may be concluded with Sherbrooke sherry nutmeg cake or lemon sponge cake with raspberries and cream. Home baking may be purchased from the bakeshop behind the dining room.

The Bright House is open mid May to mid October, (12 noon to 8 p.m.) daily. Visa and Master Card are accepted.

The Bright House
P. O. Box 97
Sherbrooke, N. S.
BOJ 3CO
(902) 522-2691

The Captain's House

The Captain's House dining room and lounge is situated on the back harbour of Chester, Nova Scotia. Originally known as Shoreham, this 1822 structure was built by New Englander Rev. John Secombe.

Superb cuisine is expertly prepared by chefs Stephen Butler and Baz Lee. The Captain's House features a large main floor dining room plus three private dining or seminar rooms on the second level, making it an ideal location for specific functions or meetings.

The Captain's House is open February though New Years, and major credit cards are accepted.

The Captain's House
Restauranteurs: Nicki and Jerry Butler
129 Central Street
Chester, N. S. BOJ 1JO
(902) 275-3501

Chez La Vigne

Chez La Vigne (The Grapevine Café), is located in the picturesque university town of Wolfville. Situated at the eastern end of the Annapolis Valley, Wolfville looks towards Cape Blomidon over miles of dykeland that runs down to the shore of the Minas Basin.

Alex Clavel, the owner-operator of Chez La Vigne, brings to your table his knowledge and expertise as an international chef. In 1989 he was chosen "Chef of the Year" by his peers at the Canadian Federation of Chefs de Cuisine.

Seafood and artful meal presentations are the specialities at Chez La Vigne. Alex grows his own herbs and uses the freshest products available. The restaurant is open year round Monday to Saturday for lunch and dinner and Sunday for dinner only. Major credit cards are accepted.

Chez La Vigne
17 Front Street
Wolfville, N. S. BOP 1XO
(902) 542-5077

The Compass Rose

The Compass Rose, close to shopping and sightseeing, is located one block from the harbourfront in the town of Lunenburg.

This provincial heritage property was built in 1825 and is a classic example of Georgian-style architecture. Operated by Suzanne and Rodger Pike as a traditional small inn with restaurant and intimate guest lounge, the Compass Rose has five bedrooms with three shared baths. The Pikes also manage the Lion Inn, a bed and breakfast at 33 Cornwallis Street, Lunenburg.

The restaurant at the Compass Rose specializes in traditional Lunenburg dishes, such as sauerkraut, as well as fresh seafood and steaks. The inn and restaurant are open daily mid February to December 5 for breakfast (8 to 9:30 a.m.), lunch (11:30 a.m. to 2:30 p.m.) and dinner (from 5 p.m.). Major credit cards are accepted.

The Compass Rose
Innkeepers: Rodger & Suzanne Pike
15 King Street
Lunenburg, N. S. BOJ 2CO
(902) 634-8509

Cooper's Inn

Located in a wonderfully restored, 18th-century waterfront home, this weathered inn offers accommodations in three guestrooms with private baths. The owners have just received the Built Heritage Award from Heritage Trust Nova Scotia for their restoration of the circa 1785 inn.

The dining room is open Monday through Saturday, serving lunch from 12 noon to 2 p.m. and dinner between 5:30 and 9 p.m.

At Cooper's Inn dining out is considered entertainment. The atmosphere is relaxed yet with expert service that ensures a comfortable ambience so guests may linger over coffee and conversation. Open year round, the inn accepts Visa, Master Card and American Express.

Cooper's Inn
Innkeepers: Gary & Cynthia Hynes
Dock Street and Mason Lane
P. O. Box 959
Shelburne, N. S. BOT 1WO
(902) 875-4656

The Galley

The Galley, part of the South Shore Marine complex, overlooks picturesque Marriott's Cove in Nova Scotia's Mahone Bay.

The nautical decor of this fine restaurant carries over to the adjacent Tic-O-Fog Lounge and aptly named giftshop, the Loft. In addition, South Shore Marine provides special meeting facilities and a boardroom with seating for 18. The Galley features homemade soups and chowders, summer salads, the freshest of seafoods, several different entrées and sumptuous desserts.

Whether you arrive by auto or by sea vessel and moor at the marina, the Galley promises the splendour of an Atlantic sunset for your own personal reflection and enjoyment. The Galley is open seasonally, March 15 through December 15, with major credit cards accepted.

The Galley
Marriott's Cove
P. O. Box 316
Chester, N. S. BOJ 1JO
(902) 275-4700

The Garrison House Inn

The Garrison House Inn is located in Annapolis Royal, Canada's oldest permanent settlement. Founded in 1605 by Samuel de Champlain, the town and its environs are steeped in history and offer visitors museums, live theatre, historic gardens, golf and touring. Also nearby is the provincially-operated Upper Clements Theme Park.

The inn itself is a restored heritage property, originally built in 1854 as the Temperance Hotel. It currently offers seven bedrooms, five with private bath and two shared.

A licensed dining room offers breakfast to guests and dinner to guests and the general public. Major credit cards are accepted and the inn operates seasonally, May 1 to November 1.

The Garrison House Inn
Innkeeper: Patrick Redgrave
P. O. Box 108
Annapolis Royal, N. S. BOS 1AO
(902) 532-5750

Gowrie House

Gowrie House was constructed in 1830 for a Mr. Archibald, the agent general of the General Mining Association. His melancholy wife named it after her home, Blair Gowrie, in Scotland. Homesick though they may have been, the Archibalds became permanent Canadians and their family maintained the home until 1975, when it was purchased by present owner Clifford Matthews.

Each of the six guestrooms has been furnished with carefully chosen antiques and decorated to enhance the feeling of comfortable elegance. Full country breakfast is served each day and is included in the rate for the room. Dinner is served to guests and the general public by advance reservation only and may include delicacies from the waters, fields and gardens of Nova Scotia.

Gowrie House is a perfect starting spot for a tour of Cape Breton. The scenic Cabot Trail, Alexander Graham Bell Museum, Miner's Museum and Fortress Louisbourg are less than an hour away.

The inn is open seasonally, May 1 to October 31, with Visa and Master Card accepted.

Gowrie House
Innkeepers: Clifford Matthews and Ken Tutty
139 Shore Road
Sydney Mines, N. S. B1V 1A6
(902) 544-1050

Halliburton House Inn

Situated on a quiet street in downtown Halifax, this centrally located inn is only a few blocks from the waterfront and the business core of the capital city. A variety of shops, fine restaurants, museums and parks are a short walk from the front door.

Built sometime between 1809 and 1860, this stone and brick building was once the home of Sir Brenton Halliburton, the first chief justice of the Supreme Court of Nova Scotia. The inn actually incorporates three registered heritage townhouses, each impeccably restored to its former elegance and decorated appropriately in period antiques.

The inn features 34 guestrooms with private baths and offers patrons afternoon tea and a complimentary buffet breakfast. The dining room is open to guests and the general public for dinner from 6:30 to 9:30 p.m., seven days a week. Master Card, Visa, American Express and En Route are accepted. Reservations are recommended.

The Halliburton House Inn
Innkeepers: Charles Lief & William McKeever
5184 Morris Street
Halifax, N. S.
B3J 1B3
(902) 420-0658

Harbourview Inn

Harbourview Inn is located on the shores of the Annapolis Basin at Smith's Cove, Nova Scotia. It is a relaxing inn, surrounded by pleasant gardens, and offers guests tennis, an outdoor pool and leisurely strolls along the seashore.

The immediate area offers visitors a variety of daytrips, such as historic Annapolis Royal and Port Royal, the colourful Acadian "French Shore" and whale watching on Digby Neck.

Harbourview Inn has nine rooms (one family suite), all with private baths and either ocean or garden views. The inn is open seasonally, June 15 to October 15, and accepts Visa and Master Card.

Harbourview Inn
Innkeepers: Philip & Mona Webb
P. O. Box 35
Smith's Cove, N. S.
BOS 1SO
(902) 245-5686

Inn on the Lake

Conveniently located 10 minutes from the Halifax International Airport en route to the cities of Halifax and Dartmouth, the Inn on the Lake is a small country club hotel set on five acres of parkland at the edge of beautiful Lake Thomas.

Guests are invited to use the free shuttlebus service to the airport as well as tennis courts, shuffle boards, jogging trails, white sand beach, heated outdoor pool, wind surfers, paddleboats and much more.

Award-winning chef Roland Glauser presents a menu following a seasonal theme, using the very best of ingredients and local produce. Dining is offered in the main dining room, on the terrace, by the gazebo bar in the park and in Oliver's Pub.

Breakfast, lunch and dinner are served daily from 7 a.m. until 11 p.m. All major credit cards are accepted.

Inn on the Lake
P. O. Box 29 (Highway 102 & 118, exit 5)
Waverley, N. S. BON 2SO
(902) 861-3480

The Innlet Café

The Innlet Café is one of a group of retail establishments located in the provincial heritage property Kedy's Landing. Comprised of three buildings – the Alexander Kedy II House, The Pine Cottage and The Warehouse – this complex lies at the end of the harbour overlooking the water and picturesque town of Mahone Bay.

Owned and operated by Jack and Katherine Sorenson, the Innlet Café specializes in seafood, chowders, home baked goods and dinner plates.

The café is open July and August daily (10 a.m. to 8 p.m.), Sunday (noon to 8 p.m.) and from September to June daily (10 a.m. to 5 p.m.) and Sunday (noon to 5 p.m.).

The Innlet Café
Restauranteurs: Jack & Katherine Sorenson
R R # 2 Kedy's Landing
Mahone Bay, N. S. BOJ 2EO
(902) 624-6363

Inverary Inn Resort

A touch of Scotland is found at Inverary Inn Resort in Cape Breton. Situated at Baddeck, with private frontage on beautiful Bras d'Or Lake, the resort features 116 motel-type units, five housekeeping cottages, four non-housekeeping cottages and The Patch Quilt Gift Shop. Playgrounds, in and outdoor pools, sauna, tennis courts, exercise room, meeting and banquet facilities make this an ideal destination.

The dining room serves such specialities as bannock, Scottish oatcakes, smoked salmon and a variety of meat and seafood entrées. The resort is open year round and major credit cards are accepted.

Inverary Inn Resort
Innkeeper: Scott MacAuly
P. O. Box 190
Baddeck, N. S. BOE 1BO
(902) 295-2674

Keltic Lodge

"My dear, that is the place!" So spoke Henry Corson in the late 1800s on first viewing Middle Head, the present site of Keltic Lodge. The Corsons, from Akron, Ohio, had been advised to find a healthier environment for Mrs. Corson, who had tuberculosis. Within the year Middle Head was purchased, a large log home built, orchards planted and a thriving dairy farm established.

Today the Corson's home has been replaced by the main lodge at Keltic but the ocean, the mountains and the clear, unpolluted air still identify it as "the place" the Corsons saw nearly a hundred years ago.

Keltic Lodge is now operated by the Province of Nova Scotia. From mid December to mid March, the White Birch Inn offers lodging and gourmet dining. The complete complex is open from June to mid October and offers convention services, saltwater pool, tennis courts, championship golf course, lodging and European cuisine.

Keltic Lodge
Ingonish Beach, N. S. BOC 1LO
(902) 285-2880

La Perla

La Perla, with the adjacent San Remo room, is located in the heart of downtown Dartmouth, only a minute's walk from the ferry linking the sister city of Halifax.

Noted for its northern Italian cuisine, owner Pearl MacDougal oversees the preparations of dishes ensuring the use of only the freshest of ingredients.

The restaurant is open daily: the San Remo Room for lunch and dinner, Monday to Friday (11 a.m. to 1:45 p.m. and 5 to 9:45 p.m. La Perla dining room serves dinner only during the above hours and on Saturday and Sunday (5 to 9:45 p.m.). Visa, Master Card, Diners and EnRoute Cards are accepted. Reservations are suggested.

La Perla Restaurant
71 Alderney Drive
Dartmouth, N. S. B2Y 2N7
(902) 469-3241 or 464-1223

Liscombe Lodge

Liscombe Lodge, situated 100 miles from Halifax on Nova Scotia's eastern shore, rests on the banks of a rolling river and offers full service with a relaxed, easy-going atmosphere.

The resort consists of 15 private chalets, five four-bedroom cottages and 30 lodge rooms. There is a marina, tennis courts, children's playground, hiking trails, canoe rentals and guide services. A nearby attraction is Sherbrooke Village, a living museum that takes you back to the mid 1800s when the village was a major lumbering and shipbuilding centre.

Dining in an enclosed verandah among nature's finest backdrop is a unique experience. A house speciality is smoked fish, prepared from an old Micmac recipe, and cured in an outdoor pit in full view of waiting diners.

Liscombe Lodge is open seasonally, May 1 through November 1, and major credit cards are accepted.

Liscombe Lodge
Liscomb Mills, N. S. BOJ 2AO
(902) 779-2307
Winter address:
P. O. Box 456
Halifax, N. S.
B3J 2R5

The Lunenburg Inn

The Lunenburg Inn is a charming turn-of-the-century home offering six guestrooms and a dining room featuring the best in traditional Nova Scotian and Mediterranean dishes.

The inn, known during the 1920s prohibition days as the Hillsdale Hotel, became the gathering place of Lunenburg's gentry. It is even rumoured that rum runners made secret deals and planned dark-of-night deliveries in the upper rooms.

Today innkeepers Faith and John Piccolo offer their guests elegant accommodations, fine food, charter arrangements, sports equipment rentals and tours of the area. The dining room is open to the public daily (5 to 10 p.m.) in season and during weekends off season. Major credit cards are accepted.

The Lunenburg Inn
26 Dufferin Street
P. O. Box 1407
Lunenburg, N. S.
BOJ 2CO
(902) 634-3963

The Manor Inn

The Manor Inn is a gracious structure, nestled amid nine acres of flowered landscape at the edge of Doctor's Lake in Hebron, Nova Scotia. The inn is close to Yarmouth International Ferry Terminal, the airport and highways 101 and 103.

Once the estate of the late H. H. Raymond, the inn is colonial in style. Its interior reflects the elegance of the early 1900 period, including a staircase of South American mahogany and several fireplace mantel pieces of carved Wedgewood.

The complex consists of the inn with six guestrooms, a coach house offering four units and adjacent motel-style accommodations. House specialities in the dining room include prime rib, fresh lobster and other taste-tempting delights from the land and sea.

The resort is open year round and major credit cards are accepted.

The Manor Inn
Innkeepers: Bev & Terry Grandy
P. O. Box 56
Hebron, Yarmouth Co., N. S.
BOW 1KO
(902) 742-2487

The Maple Inn

The Maple Inn is a charming counry inn located in the town of Parrsboro, N. S. on the shores of the Bay of Fundy. Two century-old houses have been renovated and joined to provide eight tastefully decorated guest rooms and a sitting room with fireplace.

The dining room specializes in homecooked dishes, many of which are prepared from local ingredients like maple syrup, strawberries and blueberries. Reservations are required by 2 p.m. for diners who are not guests of the inn. Dinner is served daily at one sitting.

The Maple Inn is open year round and is close to live summer theatre, golf and beaches that are world famous for their fossils and semi-precious stones. Visa, Master Card and American Express cards are accepted.

The Maple Inn
Innkeepers: Bruce & Kathleen Boles
P. O. Box 247
Parrsboro, N. S.
BOM 1SO
(902) 254-3735

Milford House

Built originally in the 1860s as a "halfway house for travellers," Milford House has been providing food, lodging and a peaceful retreat for outdoor enthusiasts ever since.

Milford House offers guests a naturalist's lifestyle. Twenty-four cottages are situated on two lakes, all private yet within walking distance of the main lodge and dining room. Each cottage has its own lakeside dock, fireplace and two to five bedrooms. Guests enjoy tennis, croquet, volleyball, swimming, a children's play area, canoeing and hiking on 600 acres of woodland.

Meals in the dining room feature wholesome country cooking using the area's freshest fruits, vegetables and seafoods and home baked breads.

The lodge is open mid June to mid September with two winterized housekeeping cottages for off-season and winter use.

Milford House
South Milford
R R # 4 Annapolis Royal, N. S.
BOS 1AO
(902) 532-2617

Mountain Gap Inn

The year 1990 marks the 75th anniverary of Mountain Gap Inn, located on the edge of the Annapolis Basin at Smith's Cove, N. S.

This inviting resort has 114 rooms, including cottages and family units overlooking the water (some with private verandahs), plus spacious motel and efficiency units. The large waterfront dining room features fresh seafood and traditional Nova Scotian dishes, served while patrons relax before a blazing fire.

Mountain Gap Inn has a beach, swimming pool, outdoor chess, tennis courts, licensed pub and patio, plus 45 acres of gardens and natural woodlands to roam. Whale and seabird-watching charters may be arranged.

Open seasonally, May 1 through October 31, the inn accepts Visa, Master Card, American Express and EnRoute.

Mountain Gap Inn
P. O. Box 40
Smith's Cove, Digby Co., N.S.
BOS 1SO
(902) 245-2277 or (902) 245-5840

The New Consulate Restaurant

The New Consulate Restaurant in Pictou, Nova Scotia, derives its name from the fact that the building housed the American Consulate during the latter half of the 19th century.

A provincially designated historic property, The New Consulate was originally built in 1827 in traditional Scottish townhouse fashion.

The fully licensed restaurant serves European and Canadian cuisine. It operates year round, May through September daily (11:30 a.m. to 11 p.m.), October through December from Tuesday to Sunday and January through April, Wednesday to Saturday, dinner only.

The New Consulate Restaurant
Restauranteurs: Floyd & Claudette Brine
115 Water Street
Pictou, N. S.
(902) 485-4554

The Normaway Inn

The Normaway Inn has been a resting spot for salmon anglers and travellers since 1928. Beautifully situated on 250 acres in the Margaree Valley of the Cape Breton Highlands, the Normaway offers a unique experience in true Cape Breton hospitality.

Whether your interest is angling on one of North America's finest salmon and trout rivers or exploring the beauties of nature through photography, hiking or touring, the Margaree will satisfy your desires. A short drive down the Valley will find you on the Gulf of St. Lawrence with its expansive white beaches and deep sea fishing.

The inn offers nine bedrooms with a common living room in the main lodge as well as four two-room cabins and 14 one-bedroom cabins.

Meals are served to guests and the general public in the dining room where you can experience country cooking with a hint of the gourmet. Innkeeper David MacDonald specializes in using the finest local products, such as lamb, salmon and produce from the inn's garden.

The Normaway also offers guests tennis, bicycles and live entertainment in the Gaelic tradition.

The inn is open seasonally, June 15 to October 15, accepts major credit cards and offers M.A.P. or E. P. accommodations as well as special honeymoon and fishing packages.

The Normaway Inn
Margaree Valley, N. S.
BOE 2CO
(902) 248-2987 or 1-800-565-9463 toll free

O'Carroll's Restaurant

O'Carroll's Restaurant and Lounge, located at 1860 Upper Water Street, is in the heart of Halifax's restored waterfront district.

Host Jim O'Carroll brings years of experience in the restaurant business from Glasgow, Scotland and offers patrons classic dishes with a variety of Scottish specialities. A weekly favourite is the Gaelic-Irish soup Brotchan Buidhe, a recipe made popular at Edinburgh's restaurant the Buttery.

O'Carroll's is open for lunch Monday through Friday, 11 a.m. to 2:30 p.m. Dinner is served Monday through Saturday, 5 to 10 p.m. American Express, Master Card, Diners and En-Route are accepted and reservations are suggested.

O'Carroll's Restaurant
1860 Upper Water Street
Halifax, N. S. B3J 1S8
(902) 423-4405

The Pines Resort Hotel

Situated high on a wooded hillside, this four-storey, Norman-style chateau is owned and operated by the Province of Nova Scotia. The Pines overlooks the Annapolis Basin and the town of Digby, N.S. The main hotel contains 85 tastefully decorated guest rooms, while 32 one, two and three-bedroom cottages with living rooms and stone fireplaces, are located nearby.

The Pines offers a 6,204-yard championship golf course, a large, heated outdoor pool, lighted tennis courts, putting green, shuffleboard, croquet courts and scenic nature trails. Succulent, artfully presented dishes are served in the hotel's Annapolis Room to guests and the general public.

The hotel can accommodate groups of up to 300 and is open seasonally, June to October, and major credit cards are accepted.

The Pines Resort Hotel
P. O. Box 70
Digby, N. S. BOV 1AO
(902) 245-2511

Silver Spoon Restaurants

Deanna Silver, owner/operator of two restaurants in the downtown area of Halifax, N. S., offers guests a fine dining experience with both her traditional and innovative fare. Specialities include homemade pasta, fresh seafood and Deanna's famous desserts, all made on the premises.

The new Silver Spoon is located at 1813 Granville Street, Halifax, N.S. B3H 1X8 (422-1519) with a café, formal dinning room and a private function room. Party trays, picnic baskets, desserts and gift items are assembled for take-out with short notice. The Silver Spoon is open year round, Monday through Saturday.

Silver Spoon Café (5657 Spring Garden Road, Park Lane Complex, Halifax, N. S., 902-422-1616) serves lunch and dinner in a café-style atmosphere. It is open year round, Monday through Saturday.

TATTINGSTONE INN

Tattingstone Inn

This elegant, English-style country inn is decorated with 18th century antiques but offers guests the modern comforts of today. A music room with grand piano, well-stocked library, tennis court, outdoor heated pool, steam room and beautiful gardens are available for guests' use.

Located in the small university town of Wolfville, Nova Scotia, visitors will find this a central location for a variety of activities – touring, photography, bird watching, arts and crafts.

The licensed dining room at Tattingstone Inn is open for breakfast to guests and open to the general public for afternoon tea and dinner. Reservations are recommended.

Open year round, the inn accepts all major credit cards.

Tattingstone Inn
Innkeeper: Betsey Harwood
434 Main Street
P.O. Box 98
Wolfville, Nova Scotia
BOP 1XO
(902) 542-7696

Telegraph House

Telegraph House

The Telegraph House on the shores of the Bras d'Or Lake in Baddeck, N. S. is steeped in Cape Breton history. It has been owned and operated since 1861 by five generations of the Dunlop family.

The inn once housed the Trans-Oceanic Cable Company, where some of North America's first telegraph messages originated (hence its name). The inn was also frequented by Alexander Graham Bell and his room, preserved in the same fashion as it was when he stayed there in the late 1880s, may be requested.

The Telegraph House is open year round and offers visitors either period rooms in the inn or modern motel units. The dining room, with its homecooked meals, specializes in traditional Maritime fare. Visa and Master Card are accepted.

The Telegraph House
Innkeepers: The Dunlop Family
Chebucto Street
P. O. Box 8
Baddeck, N. S.
BOE 1BO
(902) 295-9988

Upper Deck Restaurant

The Upper Deck Restaurant is located in the Privateers' Warehouse of Historic Properties on the Halifax waterfront.

Once the home of Enos Collins, this 200-year old structure has been home to many things, from the booty of the privateers of old to the present-day restaurant. The dining room has retained the nautical flavour of its origins with its heavy beams and ship models, including the famed schooner Bluenose.

Since its conception in 1975, the Upper Deck has gained a reputation for impeccably prepared seafood as well as beef and lamb dishes, all presented with excellent service.

The Upper Deck is open year round, serving lunch (11:30 a.m. to 2 p.m.) Monday to Friday, dinner (5:30 to 11 p.m.) Monday to Saturday, Sunday (5 to 10 p.m.). Reservations are recommended. All major credit cards are accepted.

Upper Deck Restaurant
Privateer's Warehouse
Historic Properties
Halifax, N. S.
(902) 422-1289

Victoria's Historic Inn

Built in 1880, Victoria's Historic Inn of Wolfville, N. S. was once the home of apple merchant W.H. Chase. The three-storey structure is a tribute to the craftsmanship of the 19th century. The gingerbread verandahs, sheltered entries and ornamental eaves are classic examples of Victorian architecture. The wide entrance hall and stairway are panelled with richly hued cherrywood and the second floor landing glows with the light of a beautiful stained glass window. Six of the 18 rooms contain fireplaces, each uniquely different with fruitwood, oak or marble mantels. This grand old home became an inn in 1947.

The inn is filled with antiques typical of the Victorian era. The refined atmosphere extends to the guest rooms in the main house as well as the dining rooms where country-style dinners are served. The inn is open year round and dinner is served Wednesday through Sunday, while breakfast is served to house guests daily. A coach house to the rear offers motel or cottage-style lodgings.

Victoria's Historic Inn
Innkeepers: Carol & Urbain Cryan
426 Main Street
P. O. Box 308
Wolfville, N. S.
BOP 1XO
542-5744

Zwicker's Inn

Lord Dalhousie, Lieutenant Governor of Nova Scotia in 1816 and later Governor General of the Canadas and Commander-in-Chief in India, recalled in his personal journal the frequent sojourns his family made to Prince's Harbour, the present Mahone Bay, N. S. The focal point of their visits was a country inn and tavern operated by a German settler named Zwicker.

Zwicker's Inn has been in operation sporadically since 1800, for the past 10 years as a restaurant widely known for its Nova Scotia fare. Soups, sauces, breads, noodles and ice creams are all made on the premises from fresh seafood, meats and produce.

Zwicker's is open year round, seven days a week, (11:30 a.m. to 9 p.m.), with reduced hours in winter. Major credit cards are accepted.

Zwicker's Inn
Innkeepers: The Hagreen family
662 Main Street
Mahone Bay, N. S.
BOJ 2EO
(902) 624-8045

Inns and Restaurants of Prince Edward Island

The Dundee Arms Inn

The six period guest rooms of the Dundee Arms Inn offer an atmosphere of graciousness while the Griffon Dining Room features gourmet cuisine. For those who prefer, 10 motel units are adjacent to the main lodge.

Built in 1903 in the Queen Anne Revival style, the inn was once the home of Parker Carvell, son of lieutenant governor Jedediah Cavell. The home was purchased by the current owners in 1977 who have carried out extensive restoration but endeavoured to maintain the original architectural design.

The Dundee Arms Inn is open year round and is close to the Confederation Centre of the Arts, Province House National Historic Site and the Prince Edward Island Convention Centre. American Express, Master Card, Visa or En Route are accepted.

The Dundee Arms Inn
Innkeepers: Don & Mary Clinton
200 Pownal Street
Charlottetown, P. E. I.
C1A 3W8
(902) 892-2496

The Garden Restaurant

When co-owners Jochi Schuhberger and John Alway decided to turn their farmhouse in rural Vernon River, P.E.I. into a restaurant, both gentlemen brought widely diversified talents into the venture. Austrian-born Jochi was an instructor at the Culinary Institute of Charlottetown, while John, a biologist, created the magnificent collection of plants and exotic birds that make a visit to the Garden a pleasant and restful experience.

Jochi is attentive to using the freshest of Island produce. Everything is prepared on premises, from breads, smoked meats and seafood to the fabulous array of treats on the dessert tray. The menu is extensive and Chef Jochi to calls it "country cuisine of the world."

While the food and service is superior, the view from the floor to ceiling windows of the dining room is breathtaking. Two manmade lakes, each with islands covered with perennial flowers, form a backdrop as several unique species of ducks and black and white swans drift by. In a nearby mesh enclosure peacocks strut to their feeders.

The Garden is open April to December 22 for lunch, afternoon tea and dinner daily, with brunch served Sundays. Visa and Master Card are accepted and reservations are a must.

The Garden Restaurant
Vernon River, P. E. I.
COA 2EO
(902) 651-2323

The Inn at Bay Fortune

Situated on 46 acres facing Bay Fortune as it opens out to the Northumberland Strait, the inn is just eight miles from the Magdalen Islands ferry in Souris and 45 miles from the Island's capital, Charlottetown.

Built in 1910 as a summer hideaway by playwright Elmer Harris (author of Broadway's 1940 hit "Johnny Belinda"), the inn offers 11 spacious suites, each with a view of the sea and a romantic sitting area complete with fireplace. The inn's four-storey tower includes a common room observatory and telescope.

In the Wilmer's tradition of catering to their guests' every need, the elegant dining room features fine cuisine prepared by a gourmet chef. Should you wish to explore the area or just sit on the beach, box lunches may be arranged.

The inn is open seasonally, June 15 to October 15, and the dining room serves guests and the general public. Master Card and Visa are accepted.

The Inn at Bay Fortune
Innkeeper: David Wilmer
Bay Fortune
R R # 4
Souris, P. E. I.
(902) 687-3745

Shaw's Hotel

When Great Grandfather Shaw opened an inn on the family's pioneer farm in 1860, he wanted to provide a relaxing country lodging for visitors to the Island. One hundred and twenty-nine years later, the fourth generation of the Shaw family continues this tradition.

Each of the 24 rooms in the lodge is decorated individually in a traditional Island style, some with private baths. The original farmhouse is now a suite with a large sitting room, fireplace and antique furnishings. Twelve cottages surround the inn. They feature one to four bedrooms and five have their own fireplace. In addition six new, two-bedroom cottages with kitchens, saunas or whirlpool spas, woodstove fireplaces and patio decks are located nearby. Famed Brackley Beach with its pink sand and windswept dunes is only a five-minute walk through a shaded lane from the hotel.

Shaw's American Plan includes superb meals in the daily rates. The dining room is also open to the public by reservation. Fresh Atlantic lobster or salmon, scallops, prime rib or Island lamb are but a few of the offerings from their extensive menu. American Express, Master Card and Visa are accepted. The resort is open June 1 to October 1.

Shaw's Hotel and Cottages
Innkeepers: Robbie & Pam Shaw
Brackley Beach, P. E. I.
COA 2HO
(902) 672-2022

Stanhope by the Sea

Stanhope by the Sea

Stanhope by the Sea is situated on 10 lush green acres between the sand beaches of the Gulf of St. Lawrence and Covehead Bay. Built in 1855 as Point Pleasant Lodge, this country inn was completely refurbished in 1988, using period antiques in the Prince Edward Island heritage style. In total, more than 70 units comprise this modern resort.

The dining room at Stanhope by the Sea offers a breakfast buffet and, in the evening, quality family dining featuring fresh seafood, lamb, beef and pork entrées and barbecues.

Windsurfing is a feature attraction and equipment is available onsite with instructions in French or English. An 18-hole championship golf course, guided nature walks, deep sea fishing charters, tennis and supervised ocean beaches are close by. Open seasonally, May through October 15, the inn accepts Master Card and Visa.

Stanhope by the Sea
Innkeeper: Dr. Alfy Tadros
Box 2109
Charlottetown, P. E. I.
C1A 7N7
(902) 672-2047

Victoria Village Inn

This inn, circa 1884, has won a Heritage Award for Architectural Preservation. Nestled in the little seaside village of Victoria, P. E. I., the inn offers a relaxed atmosphere that is an invitation to unwind. The four guest rooms are comfortably furnished with a collection of Canadian, New England and Victorian antiques, while the two candlelit dining rooms reflect either a Victorian mode or a country style.

The menu changes frequently and features two or three entrées. Everything is prepared by the chef who promises that nothing is deep fried. The dining room is open to the public during the summer months and to house guests only from mid September to mid June. Reservations are suggested.

Adjacent to live theatre in the summer months, a craftshop and a post office, Victoria Village Inn is open year round and accepts Visa or Master Card.

Victoria Village Inn
Innkeepers: Jacqueline & Erich Rabe
Victoria, P. E. I.
COA 2GO
(902) 658-2288

The West Point Lighthouse

Erected in 1875 and manned until 1963, the Island's tallest lighthouse now offers 10 guestrooms, including a bridal suite, as well as a licensed dining room, patio and gift shop.

This electrically-operated lighthouse is located at the south-western tip of Prince Edward Island, facing the warm waters of the Northumberland Strait. The fine red sand beach at West Point Lighthouse is part of Cedar Dunes Provincial Park, making it an ideal destination for a picnic or overnight camping.

Full breakfast, lunch and dinner are served daily at the West Point Lighthouse. House specialities include seafood chowders and lobster stew, baked goods and desserts. Open seasonally, June through September, the inn and restaurant accept Visa or Master Card.

The West Point Lighthouse
R R # 2
O'Leary, P.E.I.
COB 1VO
(902) 859-3605
(902) 859-3117 off season

Index

Temperature and Metric Conversions

Temperature

Farenheit	Celsius
200	100
250	120
300	150
325	160
350	180
375	190
400	200
425	220
450	230
475	240

Basic Measures

1/8 teaspoon	0.5 mL
1/4 teaspoon	1 mL
1/2 teaspoon	2 mL
3/4 teaspoon	4 mL
1 teaspoon	5 mL
1 1/2 teaspoons	7 mL
1 tablespoon	15 mL
2 tablespoons	25 mL
1/4 cup	50 mL
1/3 cup	75 mL
1/2 cup	125 mL
2/3 cup	150 mL
3/4 cup	175 mL
1 cup	250 mL

Weight

Pounds	Grams	Ounces
1/4 lb.	115 g	4 oz.
1/2 lb.	225 g	8 oz.
1lb.	450 g	16 oz.